Concepts of
Object-Oriented
Programming

Programming Titles from McGraw-Hill

Concepts of Object-Oriented Programming

David N. Smith

IBM T J Watson Research Center
Hawthorne, NY

McGraw-Hill, Inc.
New York St. Louis San Francisco Auckland Bogotá
Caracas Hamburg Lisbon London Madrid
Mexico Milan Montreal New Delhi Paris
San Juan São Paulo Singapore
Sydney Tokyo Toronto

Library of Congress Cataloging-in-Publication Data

Smith, David N.
   Concepts of object-oriented programming / David N. Smith.
     p. cm. -- (McGraw-Hill series on programming languages)
   Includes bibliographical references and index.
   ISBN 0-07-059177-6
   1. Object-oriented programming. I. Title. II. Series.
   QA76.64.S578 1991
   005.1--dc20   91-16717
                                                    CIP

   3 4 5 6 7 8 9 0 DOC/DOC 9 8 7 6 5 4 3

ISBN 0-07-059177-6

The sponsoring editor for this book was Neil Levine. This book was set in New Century Schoolbook, Helvetica, and Courier.

Printed and bound by R. R. Donnelley & Sons Company.

Smalltalk-80 is a trademark of ParcPlace Systems, Inc.
Smalltalk/V is a trademark of Digitalk, Inc.
Macintosh is a trademark licensed to Apple Computers.
XEROX is a trademark of the XEROX Corporation.
Other trademarks are the property of their respective owners.

For subscription information to BYTE magazine: Call 1-800-257-9402 or write Circulation Department, One Phoenix Mill Lane, Peterborough, NH 03458 or your nearest McGraw-Hill office.

For Carol,
with whom I've spent
the best 21 years of my life.

Contents

x   Contents

Preface

There are many books on object-oriented programming for the professional programmer or designer who wants in depth knowledge.

There are no books on object-oriented programming for those that simply what to know what it is all about; that just cover the important ideas without trying to make the reader into a programmer or designer of object-oriented systems.

This book is for anyone who wants to understand the key concepts of object-oriented programming whether manager or professional programmer or planner or professional in another field, or just the curious.

This is not an introduction to programming; I assume that you have some familiarity with the basic concepts of conventional procedural programming. In particular, you should have some exposure to the concepts of variable, type, assignment, arrays, looping, and procedures or subroutines.

Concepts are illustrated with short programs written in the Smalltalk language. No knowledge of Smalltalk is assumed, nor is there any intent to make you into a Smalltalk programmer. However, the concepts of OOP cannot be described or understood without examples. Smalltalk, being completely object-oriented and unfamiliar to most readers, thus not bringing expectations from prior exposure, is a good learning vehicle.

Reading This Book

From time to time footnotes are used for points that assume more prior knowledge about programming.

A special type is used for programs and other computer based text.

```
If you see this
    then
        it is a computer example
end if
```

As you also may have noted, this is a personal book. You and I are both here, not as "the author" and "the reader", but as you and I, and sometimes we.

So, let us begin... .

Thanks to...

I've been working on ways to explain the concepts of object-oriented programming since 1984. This particular attempt grew from its earliest stage as a short presentation, became full day tutorials at several ACM conferences, and then evolved into various written versions.

Many people have attended the tutorials or read various versions and given me often quite frank suggestions; each of these was considered and most were adopted. I'm extremely grateful to each of these readers and students, and since I don't know all their names, I'll not mention some and omit others. Thank you one and all!

I'd like to thank several people who have provided invaluable assistance: Jim Fegen of McGraw-Hill, who first suggested making a book of my tutorial; Jerry Archibald who has increased my knowledge of OOP with numerous hours of blackboard and lunch discussions on the nature of object-oriented programming; Jeff Purdy, who encouraged me when things looked impossible; Robert Flavin, who started me down this particular path by asking for a one foil description of OOP (and who has yet to get it!); David Dykstal who provided extensive feedback; and finally R. L., who taught me about agents and publishing.

Special thanks go to my family, and especially my wife Carol, who lost me to the computer for long hours, days, and months.

Concepts of
Object-Oriented
Programming

Introduction

Object-oriented programming (OOP) is a relatively new programming technology involving concepts that are radically different from those in conventional procedural programming.

"Object-oriented" is also a fad with the term seemingly applied to almost anything. Some uses of the term are due to misunderstanding of the concepts; some are due to other technologies, such as object-oriented user interfaces, object-oriented drawing programs, object-oriented design, and object-oriented databases using the same term. However, some are pure hype with vendors trying to stir some spice into otherwise ordinary products.

Direct manipulation systems have objects such as icons or graphical shapes on the screen. Users interact with these objects directly. Since the user's interaction is with the objects, the systems are sometimes called object-oriented. There is no conceptual connection between these interactive objects and object-oriented programming. OOP is sometimes used to implement these object-oriented interfaces, thus extending the possibilities for confusion.

Object-oriented Programming

Object-oriented programming is a new way to think about programs and their structure and a new way to write programs. It is a programming technology, not a user interface or database technology. OOP has no visual component; it is not a visual language nor does it imply any kind of visual interface.

OOP is a programming technology with a specific definition and a specific set of features. The next chapter will enumerate these features, and the rest of the book will describe and illustrate them.

Smalltalk

This book introduces object-oriented programming using the Smalltalk language. Some OOP languages such as C++™[1] or Objective-C™[2] are hybrids of OOP and procedural concepts. Because they mix procedural and object-oriented concepts, hybrids make it harder for a beginner to learn just about the new concepts.

Smalltalk[3] is an entirely new language built for OOP. It was developed at XEROX™ PARC in the 1970s and early 1980s. It contains all of the concepts that are a part of OOP; more importantly, it is built entirely with object-oriented programming concepts. As a result, Smalltalk comes with a large set of ready-made objects, which are used in the construction of the language implementation and programming interface. These objects are quite general and quite useful in most new objects.

Even if you intend to program with a hybrid language, Smalltalk is the place to start since it teaches what an object is, how you design with them, how objects relate to each other, and what general purpose objects look like. In Smalltalk you must write objects; you have no choice. In a hybrid language one can write objects, but only if you know what an object is. Nothing forces you to make objects, or even guides you toward objects.

Where OOP Came From

Major changes in technology do not happen overnight. OOP traces it's lineage back to at least the late 1960s in Simula-67.[4] The concepts in Simula-67 influenced work at XEROX Palo Alto Research Center (PARC) in the early 1970s leading to Smalltalk-72, Smalltalk-76, several versions of Smalltalk-80[5,6], and the independently developed Smalltalk/V[7]. A parallel OOP development occurred at MIT[8].

The concepts in OOP have evolved across these 25 or more years mainly out of sight of the mainstream of computing systems development. The terminology that evolved along with the concepts adds to the appearance of a great difference from conventional programming.

The first real exposure of the new ideas to the world happened in the now classic August 1981 *Byte* magazine, which was dedicated to Smalltalk-80. This was followed by the "Blue Book," *Smalltalk-80: The Language and its Implementation,*[9] published in 1983, the first of a series of books from the implementers of Smalltalk at XEROX PARC. (The "Blue Book" has been replaced by the "Purple Book," *Smalltalk-80: The Language.*[10])

In 1986, ACM started a series of conferences on Object-Oriented Programming Systems, Languages and Applications (OOPSLA), which in 1990 attracted over 2000 people to technical papers, tutorials, demonstrations, and a product exposition.

Introducing Objects

Chapter 1 introduces the basic characteristics of objects and of object-oriented programming. The four basic concepts of OOP are described and illustrated with examples.

Chapter 2 presents two examples of objects and sketches the implementation of one using a pseudo-code language.

Chapter 3 introduces the Smalltalk language and compares a Smalltalk implementation of one of the examples from Chapter 2 with the pseudo-code version.

Chapter 4 compares conventional programming with object-oriented programming. A sort subroutine written in a C-like language is compared with one written in Smalltalk. Examination of the execution of the subroutine illustrates how object-oriented programming differs so fundamentally.

1

Characteristics

Object-oriented programming (called OOP for short) has a precise definition. It is easy to see if a given programming system is object-oriented or not.[11]

However, many systems having nothing to do with object-oriented programming use the term "object-oriented," often meaning something quite different.

Object-oriented programming is a programming technology only. It has no visual component, although it is often used for building graphical user interfaces. Object-oriented programming is a technology for designing and structuring programs.

To fully qualify as object-oriented, a programming language must have four characteristics:

Data hiding
Data cannot be accessed except through code associated with the data. Data hiding is sometimes called *encapsulation* because the data and its code are put together in a package or "capsule."

Hierarchy of object definitions
New objects are defined by first finding a general concept and then refining the concept into a hierarchy of definitions. Definitions lower in the hierarchy are said to inherit from definitions above, and this characteristic is called *inheritance*.

Multiple routines with the same name
Each object has procedures or subroutines associated with it. Subroutines are called *methods* in OOP. Each of these methods has a name and these names can be the same as method names in other objects. This characteristic is sometimes called *polymorphism*, which simply means multiple names.

Single type
Any variable can hold anything, and might hold different things at different times in the execution of the program.[12]

Some languages are called object-oriented when they have only some of these characteristics, or when some of these characteristics are only partly implemented.

Data Hiding (Encapsulation)

Encapsulation means that data and the code that manipulates it are defined together, and that the data cannot be separated from or accessed separately from the associated code. Those portions of a program that are not a part of a given definition cannot access any of the data in the definition. The data is thus considered encapsulated within the code.

A collection of data and its associated subroutines (methods) is called an object.

Since data and code are bound together, it does not make sense to talk about running code separately from its data. Thus running a subroutine by itself cannot be done, but running a subroutine associated with some specific data, or object, can be done.

There is a new term for invoking a subroutine of a given object. One is said to "send the object a message." The "message name" is really the name of the subroutine.

Encapsulation is also a characteristic of some languages (such as Modula-2 and Ada™) which are not object-oriented.

Examples

Objects can be things, concepts, relationships, actions, or whatever you can conceive of, write code for, and identify data for. These might include a car engine or a sales call record. The following list shows two objects, some possible methods, and some possible data.

Object:	car engine
Methods:	adjust throttle
	adjust choke
Data:	revolutions per minute
	fuel flow
	air flow
	exhaust temperature
	oil pressure
	water temperature and pressure
	engine status (running, off, cranking)

Object:	sales call record
Methods:	print record
Data:	customer
	date and time
	person seen
	results

Hierarchy of Object Definitions

Most object-oriented languages define a new object by writing a *class*. Each class holds the code and the definition of the data for a single kind of object.

Classes usually relate to some real world thing, or to concepts. In either case it is typical that the things or concepts can be defined in increasing detail, from general (e.g., *a thing that moves*), to more specific (*wheeled things* or *flying things*), to even more specific (*highway vehicle* or *bird*), and even more specific (*1990 Honda Accord LX Sedan* or *Tufted Titmouse*).

This expansion of concepts from general to specific is reflected in a hierarchy of definitions. Things that are specific to an abstraction level are defined; as the levels become more specific, new characteristics (data and code) can be added. Finally, at the lowest level, a working definition of something is achieved.

The hierarchy of definitions is one of the more powerful concepts in OOP. It forces thinking about structure early in the design process. It forces thinking about generality and concepts. It provides, in ways we'll see later, significant code sharing and reuse.

All things that can be rented in a video store have some common characteristics, such as what it is, how much per day, to whom rented (or is it in the store), when bought, how many times rented, to whom, etc.

This is captured in the concept of Video Store Rental Inventory. (Hierarchies will be shown in an outline form where indentation means that the indented item is lower in the hierarchy.)

The top concept is the rental inventory which would have data such as price of equipment,

```
Video Store Rental Inventory
    Recorded Media
        Video
            Video Tapes
            Video Disks
        Computer Games
    Equipment
        Video Recorders
        Computer Game Consoles
```

where it currently is, the manufacturer of the product, etc.

Under that is both recorded media and equipment. Each of these is a part of the rental inventory and would inherit any characteristics thereof.

Recorded media has its own characteristics: name of thing recorded, publisher, etc. Since Recorded Media is below Video Store Rental Inventory, it includes all of the concepts (as embodied in code and data) from Video Store Rental Inventory. Recorded media is further broken down into videos and games.

Videos might have recording method (Beta or VHS), artist, date recorded, etc. Since Video is below Recorded Media, it includes all of the concepts (as embodied in code and data) from Recorded Media.

In each of these cases, concepts from one level apply to those items lower in the outline, or hierarchy, and we say that the concepts are "inherited" by those lower items from items above.

Polymorphism

In OOP the names of methods belong to individual kinds of objects. Since there can be many different kinds of objects there can be duplicate names. A ball object might have a **velocity** method and a train object might also have a **velocity** method.

Polymorphism simply means that more than one method has the same name. The methods must belong to different kinds of objects.

The decision about which routine to call can be made (by the programming system itself) at execution time (dynamic polymorphism) or at compile or link time (static polymorphism). Binding at execution is the most powerful and is the only binding in some OOP languages (such as Smalltalk).

Polymorphism isn't just to take care of accidental name conflicts, but is a powerful code structuring tool itself, as we'll see later.

Polymorphism allows calling routines to operate on a number of different (usually related) objects without having to know which are which. In conjunction with the hierarchy, polymorphism allows significant code sharing and code reuse.

Single Type

Multiple types (such as integer, float, structures, arrays, etc.) cause problems in conventional languages. Each variable, whether it be local, global, a parameter, or a member of a structure, has a specific type. It can hold only data of that type. The compiler looks at that type, and the operations performed on the variables, and generates specific machine instructions that depend on the type.

It is not possible to write a sort routine in a conventional language that sorts *any* kind of data, nor a table search routine that will search a general table, since the type of the data being operated upon must be given in the sort or search routine. One thus has sort routines for short integer, long integer, floating point, long floating point, strings, and others; and one still has to write sort routines for each other case not provided.

This is one of the reasons why so little code has been achieved in practice. Algorithms cannot be expressed without having to specify too much unimportant information, such as type.

Variables in fully object-oriented languages have a single type, an object. Any variable can thus hold any object.

Code can be written that depends only on the messages sent to an object and not to the kind of object. A sort routine may only need to compare two objects, and thus depends only on the objects having a message which performs comparisons. (Of course, the objects must be of similar types for the comparison to work.)[13]

Summary

Object-oriented programming is defined by four characteristics: data hiding, hierarchy of object definitions, polymorphism, and a single type (an object).

Each of these four characteristics is necessary for a programming system to be object-oriented. The implications of these four characteristics are profound and we will spend the rest of the book exploring them.

Procedural programming has many problems which affect its ability to produce code that can be reused or easily maintained. If you are not familiar with them, Appendix B provides a short introduction. While this appendix is not required to understand this book, it may be of help in understanding some of the motivations behind object-oriented programming and why there is so much excitement about OOP among people who have struggled with older technologies for many years.

2

Objects

Objects are everywhere: you are holding one in your hand now. It has some information (its characteristics and contents) and some things you can do to it (its operations). You can turn the pages, but not see through them. Many years ago you learned the operations of a book so well that you probably don't think of them as operations.

Automobiles are objects that have size, weight, color, and other characteristics. They have operations, such as starting, pressing the brake, turning the wheel, and pressing the accelerator pedal.

Chair characteristics include style, weight, position, and maximum load. Operations might include sit on and move.

Employees have name, age, sex, salary, Social Security number (in the USA) and dependents among others. Operations include promote, calculate pay, and add dependant.

The traditional way to program a computer has separated characteristics and operations. The characteristics were carefully made separate from the operations. In the first computers, computers had little memory for either data or programs. Programs had to be small and subroutines were developed as a way to reuse bits of code and keep programs small. Data was often read in from a tape or card, worked on, and results immediately written out. Thus data and program were seen as quite separate things.

As computers grew, and as most programs kept in memory the data they would use, the old program structuring techniques continued to be used. Data was clearly separate from code; it always had been.

Object-oriented programming does not make this distinction. Those who have never written computer programs before may well find OOP comfortable; those who have programmed before may well find OOP strange at first. It may take a while to forget the ways you have learned, and to relearn another method of programming.

In this chapter we'll explore objects in computers. We will define several objects, list the characteristics, and define the operations that might be available in a computer implementation of the object.

Parts of an Object

Objects have two parts: information and operations.

Information is sometimes called data. It tells something about the object but not how the object acts.

Operations are sometimes called instructions or programs or procedures or actions or methods. Actions tell how an object acts; what it will do when something happens.

Information

Information is something like a weight or size or count. It need not be a number: it might be a color or flavor.

A chair has a color, weight, some number of legs, style, maximum weight, whether or not it is broken (from, say, having someone too heavy sit on it), the current weight on the chair, and (sometimes) a price.

An electric stove might have weight, color, number of burners, and oven capacity.

A telephone has a richer set of characteristics including weight, position, phone number, color, style, cord length, dial or tone, and possibly a list of phone numbers that can be reached from it or that are programmed into it.

Each of these lists is arbitrary; some might not be interesting at a particular time or for a particular use. We might not want to bother remembering that a chair has four legs, or we might simply assume it and not specify it explicitly. In some circumstances, other character-istics might be important: the size of the chair; is it for an adult or child?

The information you specify in an object depends on the application of that object to a problem. Deciding this set of characteristics is a matter of design.

Actions

Some things might be fully described simply by information. Most things, however, either do something or change as things are done to them.

A bird has weight, color, species, age, sex, and many more pieces of information that describe its current state. A car loan application has lots of information, including what is written on the application form, plus its position in the process of being accepted or rejected, and the name of the person handling the application for the bank.

A bird also has activities, such as flying, landing, taking off, eating, laying eggs (depending on sex of course), and feeding young (possibly depending on sex). The actions that the bank takes toward the car loan might include reading it, evaluating the loan, and accepting or rejecting the loan.

Some unique information may be associated with various of these activities, but they are not just information; they all have some idea of process or action, or change of information. Actions deal with the evaluation and change of information (and sometimes the display of information for humans to read).

There is thus a strong coupling between information and actions; actions depend on information, actions evaluate information, actions alter information, actions deliver (return) information, and actions can create new information.

Example: A bird object

The definition of a bird object involves both the definition of the information and the definition of the actions involved.

Information:

color	the color
weight	the weight of the bird
species	the kind of bird
age	how old it is
sex	the sex

Actions:

takeoff	becoming airborne
fly	flying
land	landing
eat	taking in food
layEgg	laying eggs
feedYoung	feeding the young

Each action is some bit of code that, alone or with other actions, and with the information (data), performs some calculation or changes the variables in the appropriate way.

Defining Objects

Our ultimate purpose here is to define to a computer how to do something. This means we have to tell the computer what information an object has, and we have to tell it about the actions that the object can perform.

For now, our examples of objects are real world things. This makes it easier to think about the objects. It also makes it necessary to make decisions about what characteristics and actions are "important" and should be specified.

Many objects in OOP have no real-world counterpart. Objects might represent the idea of number, or the idea of a collection of things, or the relationships between ideas.

Whether objects represent the concrete or the abstract, we have to define the information that matters and define the actions that we need.

The information will be stored in the computer in a thing called a *variable*. The steps of an action will be given in a *method* for carrying out the action. In this section we will define the information and actions of a chair.

Variables

Computers remember data, or to be more accurate, store data, in "places" called variables. Variables have names arbitrarily given to them. Each variable name can be made long and arbitrarily funny looking, depending on the rules of the language. In Smalltalk, variables can be quite long.

```
name
bookAboutObjectOrientedProgramming
birdsAndOtherThings
sizeOfShoe
xAxisPosition
employeeName
```

Chair Variables

The characteristics of a chair might be given these variable "names":

`color`	the color
`weight`	the weight of the chair itself
`style`	the style
`isBroken`	whether or not it is broken
`curLoad`	the current weight on the chair
`maxLoad`	the maximum capacity

Some of them are simply the English words for the characteristic; some are two (and could be more) words or abbreviations stuck together. To make these easier to read, we will often capitalize leading letters of imbedded words.

These names, of course, mean nothing by themselves. There is nothing about naming a variable `color` that makes it hold just colors; likewise for `weight` holding pounds or `price` holding dollars.[14]

Methods

Methods are the instructions that specify how an object does something, or how it operates; methods tell how actions are to be performed.

A chair would seem not to have any methods since it doesn't do anything. But in a computer simulation of a chair, all of those things that we take for granted in a real chair have to be specified. If it is a fragile chair, and a real large guy sits on it, it might break. We would have to write instructions that break the chair.

Methods sometimes take input information; when a chair is to be sat upon, the weight of the person is of interest. The method would thus "take" the weight of the person; sometimes we call information that a method takes "inputs" or "parameters." (The "input" to this method is the weight).

Pseudo-language

In this chapter methods will be written in a made-up or pseudo-language rather than Smalltalk. This made-up language looks more like English than does Smalltalk.

Chair Methods

The methods for the chair object are shown in the figure *The Methods of a Chair*. When someone sits on the chair, their weight is added to the weight already on the chair; if I sit on your lap, my weight is added to yours. Thus, the `sitOn` method must be told the weight of whomever is to sit down on the chair. The second column shows that `sitOn` takes `newWeight` as an input to the method.

When someone gets off of a chair, their weight is removed. The `getOff` method takes the `oldWeight` as an input.

Method	Input	What it does
`sitOn`	`newWeight`	Put `newWeight` pounds on the chair.
`getOff`	`oldWeight`	Take `oldWeight` pounds from chair.
`initialize`	(none)	Set variables to their initial values.

The Methods of a Chair

Column one is the method name, column two shows what information the method needs when it is invoked, and the third column summarizes what the method does.

We could write:

```
ask Chair to initialize
```

to ask the chair object to perform the initialize method. Then we would write:

```
ask Chair to sitOn 50.
```

to ask (really to tell) the chair that someone weighing 50 pounds just sat on it.

Inputs to methods

Inputs to a method are variables too, but not ones that define what an object is; they, instead, temporarily hold information that a method needs. Clearly the weight of someone who is just sitting down on a chair is of interest just during the act of sitting. If we need it later, we must put it into a variable that belongs to the associated object.

We could think of the input to the method as a person and we could have the chair object remember the person object that is sitting on it.

As an alternative we could have the input to the method be just the weight in pounds or kilograms of the load that is being added to it.

The choice is typical of those that must be made when writing programs for computers. The former is more powerful: we could later ask who is sitting on the chair, who sat down on the lap of the person on the chair, and how well these people know each other. The latter is simpler and for that reason we'll use it here.

Writing Methods

Instructions (in pseudo-language) for sitting on a chair might be

```
if the new weight plus the current load
is greater than the maximum load
    then
        the chair is broken
    else
        add the new weight to the current load.
```

These instructions say to see if the current load plus the new load exceeds the capacity. If it does, then the chair breaks. If not, then the new weight is added to the current weight and remembered.

We can replace some of the English phrases with the variable names defined above. We can use + for addition and > for greater than. The instructions then become:

```
if (newWeight + curLoad) > maxLoad
   then
      the chair is broken
   else
      add newWeight to curLoad.
```

This looks somewhat less readable than English, but it says the same thing. (This still isn't Smalltalk, which looks even funnier at first. We'll get to Smalltalk in the next chapter.)

Note that the third line wasn't changed. We have a variable, **isBroken**, for telling if a chair is broken. The third line needs to be changed to put something in this variable when the chair breaks.

```
if (newWeight + curLoad) > maxLoad
   then
      put true into isBroken
   else
      add newWeight to curLoad.
```

Now, when the weight exceeds the capacity of the chair, **isBroken** is set to **true**.

(The name "**true**" is one of two special names, the other is "**false**," that are often used to keep track of information that is yes/no or on/off in nature. These values might help keep track of employee submission of forms, has a given medical test been run, or should this employee get paid by check or direct bank transfer.)

Naming methods

Since we will have more than one method, we must name the method, and we must tell what values the method needs to operate:

```
Method: sitOn needs: newWeight
if (newWeight + curLoad) > maxLoad
then
    put true into isBroken
else
    add newWeight to curLoad.
```

This says that the method tells how to sit on a chair, and needs to have the weight of whoever sits on the chair. In a similar manner we can define how to get off a chair:

```
Method: getOff needs: oldWeight
subtract oldWeight from curLoad.
```

This is much simpler; since we cannot break a chair by getting up, we don't have to check to see if the chair breaks.

We also cannot repair a chair by reducing the load, so we don't have to ever set **isBroken** to **false** after it is set to **true**.

(We probably should have made sure that the current load does not

Define: **Chair**
```
color          the color
weight         the weight of the chair itself
style          the style
isBroken       whether or not it is broken
curLoad        the current weight on the chair
maxLoad        the maximum capacity
```
Method: **sitOn needs: newWeight**
```
if (newWeight + curLoad) > maxLoad
   then
       put true into isBroken
   else
       add newWeight to curLoad.
```
Method: **getOff needs: oldWeight**
```
subtract oldWeight from curLoad.
```
Method: **initialize**
```
put       'red' into color.
put         20 into weight.
put 'kitchen' into style.
put       false into isBroken.
put          0 into curLoad.
put       1000 into maxLoad.
```

The Definition of a Chair

The variables are defined and described; these are followed by the methods written in pseudo-code.

become negative if **oldWeight** is larger than **curLoad**, but we didn't.)

Initializing chairs

Chairs do not come about inside the computer by magic; we have to tell the computer about the chair and the values of the variables. We might have a method to set each of the variables:

Method: **initialize**
```
put       'red' into color.
put         30 into weight.
put 'kitchen' into style.
put       false into isBroken.
put          0 into curLoad.
put       1000 into maxLoad.
```

(The extra spaces after **put** are there just to align the values in a column so that they are easier for a human to read. We'll do a lot of spacing just for humans, but that the computer will ignore; the placing of **then** and **else** in earlier code onto separate lines is another example of spacing text to make it easier to read.)

Using chairs

We always ask the object to do something for us. This is how object-oriented programming works. Objects are asked to do things for or to or about themselves.

We have defined a chair object and some methods. We can now use the chair by asking it to initialize itself, and to then have something weighing 100 pounds sit on it, then get up, and then have something weighing 200 pounds sit on it.

```
ask Chair to initialize.
ask Chair to sitOn 100.
ask Chair to getOff 100.
ask Chair to sitOn 200.
```

Another way to talk about this is to say we send the **initialize** message to the chair, then the **sitOn** message, then the **getOff** message, and finally the **sitOn** message again. Thinking of sending messages might seem like a frivolous and useless change in terminology, but as we get further into objects we will see that something different happens when a message is sent and there are multiple objects involved in the definition.

Messages in OOP are very much like subroutine calls in conventional languages, even counting the differences we will find later. In particular a message is synchronous; that is, the method that is sending the message is not executed until the method that executes the message is finished. Many operating systems and graphical user-interface systems have the concept of a message too, but these messages really are events that can be queued and manipulated, and are *not* the same kind of message we talk about in OOP.

Making Objects

All of our work on the chair object has given us one chair. There is one set of variables to hold information about the chair and thus just one chair. Somehow we need to have more than one chair.

We could write what we've written so far and call it chair number 1 (**Chair1**), then write another and call it **Chair2**, and so on. It would be much nicer if we could define the variables and methods just once but still have more than one chair.

Recipes for making chairs

If the definition for a chair were a recipe for making a chair, instead of the chair itself, then we could make more than one chair; we could make as many chairs as we wanted whenever we wanted.

Basically, we use a recipe to make a new thing, a chair or bird or payroll record.

The definition still has two parts, but they are subtly changed in detail:

- The list of variables becomes a list of the variables that the new object (the chair) will have when created.

- The methods become the specification of the actions that the object will have when created.

Creating and using objects then has these steps:

1) Write the recipe: the list of variables and the actions.

2) Ask the recipe to create a new object.

3) Send messages to the object created by the recipe.

A recipe is called a *class*. The recipe for an object is referred to as the *class* of the object.

An object created from a class is called an *instance of the class*, or simply *an instance*. Since all objects are created from some class, all objects are also thus instances. We will tend to use the terms instance and object interchangeably.

Classes and instances are just two of the new terms that come along with OOP. Sometimes the new terms describe something familiar, sometimes the terms look forbidding at first, and sometimes the terms describe a really new concept.

Instances and classes are new concepts but are related to the idea of a data structure definition (such as the **STRUCT** statement in C), and a particular allocation of memory made to hold the data described by that structure. The code that operates on the data, plus the data structure itself, is similar to a class, and an allocation of memory holding such a structure is similar to an instance. (In C++, this parallel holds quite true with classes being an extended form of structure.)

Chairs from classes

If the definition of chair we just wrote becomes the definition of how to make a chair, then there has to be some new way to specify that we want a chair. We might do it like this:

```
put new Chair into momsChair.
```

This says to make a new chair and to then put it into the variable **momsChair**. The variable **momsChair** now holds a chair. This value is an object. Inside the object, or somehow known to it, is the data for

```
put new Chair into bobbysChair.
tell bobbysChair to initialize.

put new Chair into sallysChair.
tell sallysChair to initialize.

put new Chair into momsChair.
tell momsChair to initialize.

put new Chair into dadsChair.
tell dadsChair to initialize.

tell bobbysChair to sitOn   30.
tell sallysChair to sitOn   45.
tell momsChair   to sitOn  115.
tell dadsChair   to sitOn  185.
```

Use of Multiple Chairs

Here we create four new chairs, initialize each, and then "simulate" a family sitting down for dinner.

a chair and the methods which define its actions.

How do we get at this data so we can use it? We don't get at it ourselves. We ask the methods to do it for us.

Data in objects is always hidden; we never can get at it from outside the methods that belong to the object. This is not a failure or deficiency of OOP, but is one of its strengths. One of the major failures of most other language types is uncontrolled access to information.

We now use the chair we just made like this:

```
ask momsChair to initialize.
ask momsChair to sitOn 100.
```

This looks just like what we did earlier, sending messages to Chair; only now the messages go to a chair object we put in a variable.

Example: Multiple chairs

Real uses of chairs involve multiple chairs. The figure *Use of Multiple Chairs* illustrates four chairs and four people sitting down.

The figure *Instances and Class* shows the class, the names of the methods, and each of the instances.

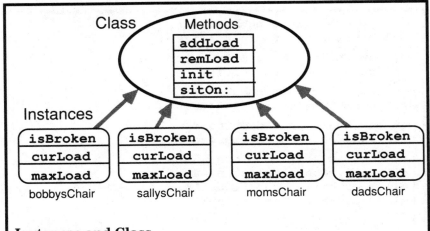

Instances and Class

This picture is similar to pictures we'll see elsewhere in the book; it shows a class as an oval with methods (here shown by just their names). Instances of the class are rounded rectangles, here showing the names of the variables held in each. The arrows show to which class the instances belong.

Memory Management

What if the value of the chair object in a variable is replaced with something else?

```
put new Chair into obj.
put new Bird  into obj.
```

First we make a new chair and put it into the variable **obj**, then we put a new bird into **obj**. What has happened to the chair?

In most conventional programming languages the memory where the chair object had been is lost. That is, we have lost track of where it is and it cannot be used for anything else until our program ends. This is not practical for anything but the most trivial problems. While it would seem simple to say when one is through with some memory, in practice much programming effort is spent keeping track of when memory can be "returned" to the pool of available memory.

In Smalltalk and some other OOP languages (and in a few specialized non-OOP languages) the language has been defined in such a way that there is no problem with lost memory. A special part of the language implementation, known as the memory management system (or "garbage collector," in programmer slang), recovers "lost" memory.

The bottom line is simple in such languages: we can forget about

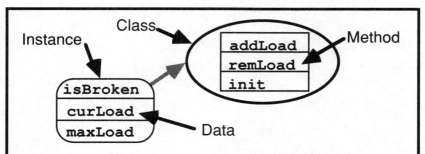

Relationship Between Class, Instance, and Method.

A class (represented by the oval) with three instance methods
has one instance (represented by the rounded rectangle) with
three instance variables. The dark arrows point to the things
named by the terms.

memory management problems. When we want a bunch of objects we
get new ones. When we are done, the system gets back the computer
memory for us.

Some other OOP languages have aids for managing memory and
some don't. In some the aids allow manual management only.

Terms

Object
A thing in a computer which has data (characteristics) and
methods (operations or actions).

Method
A subroutine which belongs to an object and which tells how to
perform some action.

Class
A recipe for building objects. It knows the variables that are in
the object and it holds the methods for each of the objects.

Instance
An object; it holds the data and a reference (pointer) to the class.
(It must have this reference to the class since the class has the
methods.)

Message
Asking an object to do something is called "sending a message."
Sending a message is similar to calling a subroutine.

3

Smalltalk

Smalltalk is about objects. In Smalltalk, almost everything is done by sending messages to objects.

This chapter will be about Smalltalk and chairs; about how to write the chair example of the previous chapter using Smalltalk.

But first, why do we want to use Smalltalk? There are several cogent reasons why you should learn OOP with Smalltalk, regardless of the language you might (or might not!) later use for production code.

Smalltalk was the first real, full OOP language. It has all the characteristics attributed to OOP. Everything is an object and there are no leftover traditional concepts or features to get in the way of learning. On the other hand, C++ is full C *plus* a major helping of OOP. It is all too easy to write just C, or extended C, but never to write an object.

Smalltalk is heavily used. Over 50 percent of the attendees at a professional conference dedicated to OOP use Smalltalk at least sometimes.[15] It is therefore used as a basis for comparison with other languages: "C++ *is like Smalltalk except ... .*"

Not the least reason for learning Smalltalk is that it runs on all but the smallest personal computers.

Besides, Smalltalk is a very small language. Its power comes from object-oriented programming and from code written in Smalltalk that provides a large reusable environment. Since the language is small, it doesn't take much to learn.

Versions of Smalltalk

Smalltalk runs on a wide variety of computers, from 1981-era IBM PCs to the most powerful workstations. There are two main dialects, one sold by Digitalk and one by ParcPlace Systems.[16]

The language is essentially the same in both versions, but, since Smalltalk is a self-extending language and is used to build its own development environment as well, the extensions and environment differ in some details.

For the purposes of this book, both versions are identical.

Variables

Smalltalk variables are just like the variables we've used so far: letters, usually words or abbreviations, stuck together to make a meaningful name. Variables can be short, like **x** or **a**, or they can be ugly like **w2j45z** or **oOoOo**, but are best when they describe what they hold, like **weight** or **birdSpecies** or **employeeName** or **size** or **numberOfElevatorBanks**.

Methods

Methods in Smalltalk look different from methods written in the language we used in the previous chapter. Each method still has a name and each still has input variables, and each still specifies actions. But beyond that, things look quite different.

The main difference is in how we ask an object to do something. Since asking objects is about all that is ever done in Smalltalk, some special thought went into how it could be done to make it easy to write and to read.

The result may not look easy at first; in fact, it may look strange. However, it is easy but it will take a bit of exposure before it all comes together and looks natural.

Asking without inputs

There are three ways to ask an object to do something. One of these we won't look at for a while yet; we'll save it until we need it. The other two are very similar to the two kinds of **ask** statement from the pseudo-language of the previous chapter. One has inputs and one does not.

Messages with no inputs are called *unary* messages. (Unary means one.) They are just like the **ask** statement where we asked an object to do something and had no inputs for it:

```
ask momsChair to initialize.
```

In Smalltalk, the object comes first followed by the name of the method:

```
momsChair initialize.
```

This does the same thing; it asks **momsChair** to run the **initialize** method. It does it without as many words to write, and it lets us send more than one message on a line, as we'll see shortly.

Asking with inputs

Methods with inputs are called *keyword* messages. They ask an object to do something, this time with inputs. We wrote:

```
ask momsChair to sitOn 50.
```

In Smalltalk, the object comes first followed by the name of the method (with a colon on it), and then the input:

```
momsChair sitOn: 50.
```

This does the same thing; it asks **momsChair** to run the **sitOn:** method. This does it without as many words to write, and it lets us send more than one message on a line, as we'll see shortly.

The colon stuck on the end of **sitOn:** is very important. It lets us (and the computer) tell the difference between a unary message and a keyword message. Without the colon

```
momsChair sitOn 50.
```

would mean to send the **sitOn** message to **momsChair** with no inputs. (The **50** would just confuse things; it would cause an error.)

Multiple inputs

Sometimes methods have more than one input. In most other languages the inputs would be grouped together inside parentheses:

```
sofa twoSitOn: (50, 35).
```

In Smalltalk, the method name is given multiple parts, one part per input:

```
sofa sitOn: 50 and: 35.
```

The method takes two inputs. (It is underscored here to make it easier to see the two parts.) There are always as many colons in the name as there are inputs. Two colons mean two inputs. The inputs go behind the colons, one colon for each input.

When the name of the method is written in text, we run the two parts together, like: **sitOn:and:** with no space between the parts.

The message name is `sitOn:and:` and is a single name, not two names, even though it is written in code in two parts.

Testing

In the last chapter, we wrote testing like this:

```
if a > b
    then
        ... things to do if true ...
    else
        ... things to do if false ....
```

In Smalltalk, testing is written like this:

```
(a > b)
    ifTrue:
        [ ... things to do if true ... ]
    ifFalse:
        [ ... things to do if false ... ].
```

The square brackets enclose one or more Smalltalk program statements. The brackets and the code they enclose is called a *block*.

Variations involving just one of the alternatives are also allowed. If only the true case is interesting, one can write

```
(a > b)
    ifTrue:
        [ ... things to do if true ... ].
```

If only the false case is interesting, one can write

```
(a > b)
    ifFalse:
        [ ... things to do if false ... ].
```

Assignment

In the last chapter, values were put into variables like this:

```
put 12 into weight.
```

In Smalltalk, the idea is exactly the same, but it is written like this:

```
weight := 12.
```

The := means to put the thing on the right side into the variable on the left. The right side can be any arbitrary Smalltalk expression; the expression is evaluated and the result is assigned, like this:

```
newWeight := weight + 2.
```

This means to take the value in the variable **weight**, add **2** to it, and put the new value into the variable **newWeight**. Or

```
weight := weight * 2.
```

means to take the value in the variable **weight**, multiply it by **2**, and put the new value into the variable **weight**.[17]

Writing methods

Earlier, we wrote a method definition like this:

```
Method: getOff needs: oldWeight
    subtract oldWeight from curLoad.
```

In Smalltalk, this is a keyword method, and will be invoked like this:

```
aChair getOff: 200.
```

The top line of the definition for **getOff:** looks like the way it is invoked:

```
getOff: oldWeight
    oldWeight := oldWeight - curLoad.
```

The first line, the definition of the name and inputs, is underscored here to help with reading. In Smalltalk, we tell that a line is the definition for a method simply because it comes first.

Periods

Statements are ended by periods, like sentences in English. However, since the last statement in a method clearly ends at the end of the method, the period is optional there. We will sometimes omit the last period in a series of statements.[18]

Classes

Recipes are called *classes* in Smalltalk and always start with an upper-case letter. Let's write the recipe for a chair in Smalltalk (see figure *Class Chair*).

Class names

The names of classes in Smalltalk always start with a leading upper-case character. All other variables start with a lower-case variable.

Thus **Chair** and **Bicycle** are classes, and **chair** and **banana** are not.[19]

New objects

In Smalltalk we get new objects by writing the name of the class followed by the word **new**.

```
Chair new
```

This has the form of a message send, sending the new message to **Chair**. (In fact, that's exactly what it is, but we'll talk more about that later.)

The example of the family sitting down to eat in Smalltalk is shown in figure *Multiple Chairs*.

Class: **Chair**

Variables:
color	the color
weight	the weight of the chair itself
style	the style
isBroken	whether or not it is broken
curLoad	the current weight on the chair
maxLoad	the maximum capacity

Methods:

<u>sitOn: newWeight</u>
```
(newWeight + curLoad) > maxLoad
    ifTrue:
        [isBroken := true]
    ifFalse:
        [curLoad := newWeight + curLoad].
```

<u>getOff: oldWeight</u>
```
oldWeight := oldWeight - curLoad.
```

<u>initialize</u>
```
curLoad   := 0.
color     := 'red'.
weight    := 20.
style     := 'kitchen'.
isBroken  := false.
curLoad   := 0.
maxLoad   := 1000.
```

Class Chair

A list of the variables in class Chair and the methods written in Smalltalk.

```
bobbysChair := Chair new.
bobbysChair initialize.

sallysChair := Chair new.
sallysChair initialize.

momsChair:= Chair new.
momsChair initialize.

dadsChair := Chair new.
dadsChair initialize.

bobbysChair sitOn: 30.
sallysChair sitOn: 30.
momsChair   sitOn: 30.
dadsChair   sitOn: 30.
```

Multiple Chairs

Here we create four new chairs, initialize each, and then "simulate" a family sitting down for dinner. This version is written in Smalltalk.

Expressions

Arithmetic and logical expressions in Smalltalk look just like expressions in other languages, and about like in algebra. We have already seen one expression:

```
newWeight + curLoad
```

The + above is also a message send; it sends the + message to the object in **newWeight** passing the object in **curLoad** as an input. It might be thought of as being like this:

```
newWeight add: curLoad
```

except that a plus sign replaces the keyword **add:**.

When the name of a method is a special character, the message is called a *binary message* because it always has two objects (the left one and the right one) and binary means two.

If the objects are numbers, the expression returns the sum of the two objects.

Another expression we've seen is

```
(newWeight + curLoad) > maxLoad
```

The addition is the same and is done first; the result of the addition can be thought of as replacing what it was calculated from:

```
result > maxLoad
```

This is now another message to send; the **>** message is sent to the object in *result*, passing **maxLoad** as an input. This returns a true or false value.

While Smalltalk does have a defined order for evaluating expressions, it is not the same as algebra, and not the same as in most other languages (none of which do it the same as any of the others anyway). Since the exact order of evaluation is not always obvious to the untrained eye, parentheses will be used in this book to show the order of evaluation, even when not strictly needed. Thus we will always write, say, **(2*3)+4** even though the parentheses are redundant.[20]

Returning values

Methods often need to calculate a value and return it. We might want to ask a chair how much load it has on it.

```
currentLoad
    ^ curLoad
```

This method is named **currentLoad**. It simply returns the value of the **curLoad** variable. The caret[21] just in front of the variable name means to take the value that follows, stop the current method, and continue with the previous method using the value as the result. That is, the value after the caret is returned as the value of this method.

It is by returning values that we can safely expose values to the outside world. Why is this safe? For several reasons:

1) We can, at any time, take away the method (after all it is ours) and stop others from accessing the variable's value.

2) We can, at any time, add code to the method to make sure that values are proper, or to perform other calculations to find the value (or track who is using the value). This often is necessary as a program changes across time.

Looping

There are many ways to write loops in Smalltalk. Some involve messages to collections, such as arrays, asking the collection to evaluate a block for each object it contains. Later on, we'll look further at this kind of looping.

Loops that parallel constructs in conventional languages can also be written.

First, simply looping for a given number of times:

```
i := 0.
10 timesRepeat: [
    i := i + 1.
    (do something with i)
    ]
```

Next, looping with an index set to a value. This is equivalent to the **for** loop in C or the **DO** loop in FORTRAN.

```
0 to: 10 do: [ :i |
    (do something with i)
    ]
```

The index variable is written inside the block, at the front, and has a colon on the front (for historic reasons). The index variable is followed by a vertical bar and then one or more statements.

Looping can be from high to low too:

```
10 to: 0 by: -1 do: [ :i |
    (do something with i)
    ]
```

In each case the body of the loop is a block, just as were the true and false actions of **ifTrue:ifFalse:**.

Protocol

A protocol of an object is the list of messages to which it responds, or (equivalently) the list of methods implemented for it.

The word protocol serves to emphasize that the methods are not a hodge-podge of routines just stuck there, but serve as a method or medium of discourse.

Sometimes the term protocol refers to a coherent subset of the messages of an object, especially when several objects may have the same subset. If there are several objects that can be displayed on a screen, each may have **display**, **position**, and **size** methods. One might then refer to the "display protocol" that these objects share.

Blocks

A block is a set of one or more Smalltalk statements enclosed within square brackets:

```
[ a := b * 2 ]
```

or:

```
[ a := city populationDensity.
  b := a * (city area). ]
```

Blocks are used in testing (such as **ifTrue:**):

```
(a < b)   ifTrue: [a := a + 1 ].
```

or:

```
(city size < 100000)
    ifTrue:  [ cityType := 1 ]
    ifFalse: [ cityType := 2 ]
```

or for looping:

```
10 timesRepeat: [ screen drawBall ]
```

Comments

Comments in Smalltalk are enclosed in double quote marks:

```
(a > b) ifTrue: [ ^ a ].    "found highest value"
```

Summary

We have surveyed the basics of writing Smalltalk. We've seen how variables are written, how methods are invoked and written, how tests and if statements are written, how assignments to variables are done, how classes are defined, what expressions look like, and how values are returned from methods.

While there is more to Smalltalk, this is enough to get us started writing real code.

Terms

Binary messages
Messages with one or two special characters as the name and which always have one input value:

```
a + b
```

Send the + message to the object in the variable **a** passing the object in the variable **b** as an input value.

Block
A set of one or more Smalltalk statements enclosed within square brackets. Blocks are used in if statements and for looping.

Class
The name for a recipe in Smalltalk; the definition of data and its associated code.

Keyword message
Messages with one or more inputs. The name of the message

always ends with a colon; multiple colons indicate multiple input values.

    `city` **`population:`** `size`

Send the **`population:`** message to the object in the variable `city` and pass the object in the variable `size`.

    `city` **`name:`** `s` **`country:`** `c`

Send the **`name:country:`** message to the object in `city` and pass the objects in `s` and `c`.

Protocol

1) The list of methods belonging to a class. The protocol of an object is the things one can send (or do to) the object.

2) A logical subset of the methods of an object.

Examples might include the display protocol of objects that can be displayed on a screen or the comparison protocol of objects that can be compared with similar objects. The objects may have other protocol that differs from that of other objects that share the subset protocol.

Unary messages

Messages with no input data:

    `city population`

Send the unary message **`population`** to the object in the variable `city`.

4

Sorting Things Out

Writing programs in Smalltalk involves, as it does in other languages, many small definitions put together to form a larger structure. In Smalltalk, the details are different; rather than subroutines and data structures to define programs, we write methods and classes to define objects.

Before looking at more classes, let's look at a single method, and compare it with a subroutine which does the same thing.

The method and subroutine will each implement a simple sort algorithm. The subroutine was initially programmed in the C language, but is presented here in a pseudo-language which is less terse than C.

As we compare the two implementations of the same algorithm, we shall see some fundamental differences that OOP brings to coding; in particular we shall see how it is that a single method in Smalltalk can be far more general than a virtually identical subroutine in a conventional language.

Sort in Pseudo-code

There are many ways to sort a set of data, the simplest often being the slowest. The program in the figure *Sort Example in Pseudo-code* implements what is called a "bubble" sort, one of the simple but slow varieties. It is written in a madeup language, or "pseudo-code," that is similar to C or Pascal.

The Sort Algorithm

The sort subroutine works by examining the data many times, each time moving the largest remaining value to the back.

The first time, it compares the first item with the second; if the first is larger, it is exchanged with the second so that the larger item ends up second. Then the second is compared with the third, again exchanging the two if the first is larger.

This continues until the last two items are compared, and exchanged if needed. The last element in the array is now the largest in the array.

The process is repeated, each time looking at one less element, since each time we move the largest remaining element to the end of the remaining data items.

Problems

The algorithm is not without its problems, regardless of what it is coded in. It is simple but slow. On large collections of data it can seemingly take forever. Many other methods for sorting are faster, and as a result this algorithm is rarely used.

Some other problems come from its having been written in a conventional language and occur regardless of details of the sort algorithm.

First (line 1), the procedure knows about the type of array to be sorted (an array of integers).

Next (line 2), the contents of the elements of the array (integers)

```
1  procedure sort( int array data, int size );
2      int temp, i, j;
3      repeat with i=size-1 to 1 by -1;
4          repeat with j=1 to i by 1;
5              if( data[j] > data[j+1] )
6                  then
7                      temp      = data[j];
8                      data[j]   = data[j+1];
9                      data[j+1] = temp;
               end if;
           end repeat;
       end repeat;
   end procedure;
```

Sort Example in Pseudo-code

The sort example in a pseudo-code similar to C. The next figure shows this same code in Smalltalk.

are again specified since the type of variable **temp** must be the same type. The temporary variable is used to exchange elements of the array (lines 7-9). Even if the type of temporary variable **temp** didn't need to be known, the length of the data would have to govern the length of **temp**.

Third (line 5), the language knows how to compare two elements of the data array; the integer comparison is built into the procedure.

These problems make it necessary to have a separate sort routine for every element type (and, if conventional languages had more kinds of collections than just arrays, every collection type). As a result, programmers write new sort routines, over and over, for each new application.

The Sort in Smalltalk

The figure *Sort Example in Smalltalk* shows the sort program in Smalltalk. While the syntax is different, the structure is the same.

There is a method definition (line 1) that specifies the method name **sort:** and the name of the array to sort (**data**).

There is a definition (line 2) of a local variable **temp**, and there are two nested loops (lines 3,4).

Inside the loops is a comparison (line 5), a test based on it (line 6), and a swap of two elements if the test is true (lines 7,8,9).

Some syntax differs, especially that of indexing arrays. Instead of

```
data[i]
```

we write:

```
1  sort: data
2  | temp |
3  (data size) - 1 to: 1 by: -1 do: [ :i |
4     1 to: i do: [ :j |
5        (data at: j)  >  (data at: j+1)
6           ifTrue: [
7              temp := data at: j.
8              data at: j put: (data at: j+1).
9              data at: j+1 put: temp
              ].
        ].
     ].
   ^ data
```

Sort Example in Smalltalk

The sort example in Smalltalk. The previous figure showed this same code in a pseudo-code not unlike C.

```
data at: i
```

to find the ith element of **data**. Also, instead of

```
data[j] := temp
```

we write:

```
data at: j put: temp
```

to store **temp** into **data** at the jth location. Both are messages sent to the array in **data** to get or set elements. (Remember that keyword messages have one part for each input. Thus the **at**:**put**: message not only has two inputs, but is written with the **at**: in front of one and the **put**: in front of the other.)

An important difference is the lack of any declaration of the type of the parameters or local variables. All are just objects. Any parameter or local variable can hold any object.

Other differences are inherent in the concept of message sends. The array parameter **data** is asked its size (line 3); the array is asked to index itself (lines 5, 8, 9), and the elements are asked to compare themselves (line 5).

The important issue is the set of messages implemented by objects. If an object that collects data in itself (such as an array) implements **size**, **at**: and **at**:**put**:, and if the elements in the collection respond to the message **>**, then this code will run and will sort the collection.

This sort routine could thus sort integers, floating point numbers, strings, or anything else we can put into a collection and which can be compared.

Note that this is very much true only of OOP languages that let a variable hold any object. It is not true of languages requiring that variables have types since the definition of a collection written in the language (as one wants to be able to do) must know the type of the elements of the collection. Thus in such languages one can write collection objects such as "set of integers" but not just "set."

Example: Sorting integers

This and the next section will show traces of the execution of the sort method for integer and string values in the array. The left column of figure *Executing Sort* shows the code being executed. The right column shows the data being operated upon, and sometimes a fragment of code with the data values inserted. Each trace will show the first execution of the loops only.

This trace of the execution of **sort**: is done with an array of three integers: **4**, **3**, and **2**.

	Code	Data
1	<u>sort: d</u>	*Array(4 3 2)*

3	(data size)-1 to: 1 by:-1
	   do: [:i |
		3 to: 1 by: -1
		   do: [:i |
		i = 2

4	1 to: i do: [:j |	*1 to: 2 do: [:j |* *j = 1*

5	(data at: j) >
	   (data at: j+1)
		(data at: 1) >
		   (data at: 2)
		4 > 3
		true

7	temp := data at: j	*temp := data at: 1* *temp := 4*

8	data at: j put:
	   (data at: j+1)
		data at: j put:
		   (data at: 2)
		data at: 1 put: 3
		Array is now *(3 3 2)*

9	data at: j+1 put: temp	*data at: 2 put: 4* **Array is now** *(3 4 2)*

Executing Sort

The code column shows successive statements as they are executed; the data column shows the statements with values replacing variables or expressions, and resulting data. See the text for more information.

Let's now look at what is happening, line by line.

1	<u>sort: d</u>	*Array(4 3 2)*

The sort method is invoked with an array containing three integers.

3	(data size)-1 to: 1 by:-1
	   do: [:i |
		3 to: 1 by: -1
		   do: [:i |
		i = 2

The first loop is executed. The data is asked its size (it is 3) and the loop index, **i**, will thus be **3-1** or **2**.

4	1 to: i do: [:j |	*1 to: 2 do: [:j |* *j = 1*

The second loop is executed. It will loop with the index, **j**, starting at 1.

5	(data at: j) >	(data at: 1) >
	(data at: j+1)	(data at: 2)
		4 > 3
		true

The data is asked for the elements at **j** and **j+1**. Since **j** is **1**, elements at **1** and **2** are returned. These elements are **4** and **3**.

The first element is asked to compare itself with the second (by sending it the **>** message with the second value as an input). The result of the comparison is **true**.

| 7 | temp := data at: j | temp := data at: 1 |
| | | temp := 4 |

Since the comparison was **true**, the two elements at 1 and 2 must be exchanged. The first step is to ask the array for its first element and then to put that element in the temporary variable, **temp**.

8	data at: j put:	data at: j put:
	(data at: j+1)	(data at: 2)
		data at: 1 put: 3
		Array is now (3 3 2)

Then the array is asked for the element at **2** (a **3**). The array is asked to put that value into element **1** of **data**.

Let's look at that expression in more detail. Remember that things in parentheses are done first.

The **at:** message is sent to **data** passing a **2** (which is **j+1**). That returns a value, a **3**.

Then the **at:put:** message is sent to **data**, passing two inputs. First, the value **1** (which is in **j**), and second the value **3** (which was just returned to us).

| 9 | data at: j+1 put: temp | data at: 2 put: 4 |
| | | Array is now (3 4 2) |

Finally, **data** is asked with **at:put:** to put the element in **temp** into position **2**, completing the exchange.

This process continues with the next set of elements until the largest value (a **4**) is at the end of the array. Then the code is repeated again to move the next largest element to just in front of the element **4**.

Data Independent Algorithms

Note that at no point was knowledge of the kind of data in the array incorporated into the program either by us or the language. In each case some other object, an integer or an array, was asked to do data-specific things. The same routine will sort other kinds of data, as will be seen in the next section.

	Code	Data
1	<u>sort: d</u>	<u>Array('c' 'b' 'a')</u>

3	(data size)-1 to: 1 by:-1
	    do: [:i |
		2 to: 1 by: -1
		    do: [:i |
		i = 2

4	1 to: i do: [:j |	1 to: 2 do: [:j | *j = 1*

5	(data at: j) >
	    (data at: j+1)
		(data at: 1) >
		    (data at: 2)
		'c' > 'b'
		true

7	temp := data at: j	temp := data at: 1 temp := 'c'

8	data at: j
	  put: (data at: j+1)
		data at: j
		  put: (data at: 2)
		data at: 1 put: 'b'
		<u>Array ('b' 'b' 'a')</u>

9	data at: j+1 put: temp	data at: 2 put: 'c' <u>Array ('b' 'c' 'a')</u>

Executing Sort, with Strings

The code column shows successive statements as they are executed; the data column shows the statements with values replacing variables or expressions, and resulting data. The code is unchanged from that which sorted integers.

Example: Sorting Strings

The trace of the execution of **sort**: in figure *Executing Sort, with Strings* is done with an array of three strings: **'c'**, **'b'**, and **'a'**.

Step by step the same statements are executed as with the integer case, except that the array values are strings. Since the array of strings has three elements and is in reverse order, the method will run exactly the same steps and in the same order. Only the values in the input array, and in the variable **temp** will differ.

Summary

In this chapter we wrote a small routine in Smalltalk that will sort data in an array. It does not matter what the data is, so long as it can compare itself to other like pieces of data. It does not matter what the array holds; we don't have to know. It does not even matter if the array is really an array, or some other kind of collection of data, so long as it responds to array-like indexing messages.

This example is short, and does not take advantage of several of the basic characteristics of OOP. In particular, we didn't create an object but simply a method of some unnamed and undescribed object. Yet, we've written a sort program that is far more general than we could write in any conventional non-OOP language.

OOP Concepts

Chapter 5 introduces the concept of classes, the definitional method in many OOP languages, by way of an example class. Classes contain the code of objects and a description of the data that the object will have. Alternative definitions illustrate how data hiding can be used to change an implementation without affecting the users of the class.

Chapter 6 implements a class which embodies the concept of a date.

Chapter 7 discusses and illustrates inheritance by making a class which embodies the concept of time be an extension of the one for date.

Chapter 8 describes how inheritance and polymorphism works in practice: how multiple methods with the same name can exist and how the "right one" is found.

Chapter 9 illustrates how inheritance can be used to simplify and extend the time example of Chapter 7.

Chapter 10 extends the concept of inheritance to include abstract classes which are never intended to produce real objects but are used to provide characteristics to be inherited.

5

Classes

Assume we have an object that represents a ball. It might have two variables, one to hold the mass and one to hold the velocity. It might have methods to increase the velocity or bounce the ball.

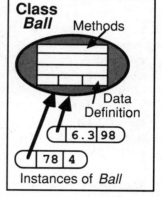

Class *Ball* Methods

Data Definition

6 . 3 | 98

78 | 4

Instances of *Ball*

Object-oriented programming systems separate the code and the definition of the data from the actual data itself.

Most OOP systems call the code and data definition a *class*. The data definition describes what the data in the object looks like; in Smalltalk, it is just a list of variable names.

The actual data is called an *instance* of the class. Each time we obtained a new Chair, we got another instance of a chair object.

Each time a new ball is needed, a new instance will have to be obtained. Each instance will hold the data for one ball.

Momentum

Moving things have a property called *momentum*. If you wish, you can simply not worry about what it is and consider it a magic number we will store and retrieve.

Momentum is a physical quantity which combines the speed, direction, and mass of balls and other moving objects. It is useful because when something bounces, its momentum doesn't change; more accurately the total momentum in a collision doesn't change, although afterwards a given ball may have more or less. This "conservation" of momentum across collisions makes it useful when determining what happens when two things bump.

Momentum is obtained by multiplying velocity by mass. Velocity is a physical quantity that combines direction and speed. It thus has both a number for speed and another for direction of travel.

In this chapter we will pretend, in order to keep things simple, that velocity has no direction and is a simple number. Our physicist friends will just have to grit their teeth.

Defining a Ball Class

A Ball class will be defined with two instance variables, for mass and velocity, and methods to allow access to the variables by the users of the class. (See box at right.)

First, the class is named: **Ball**. Then it is given two variables, **m** and **v**, for mass and velocity. Then come the methods; each method header is underlined for ease of reading. The body of the method follows immediately.

Since there is no external way to access variables that belong to an object, it is necessary to write methods to allow such access when it will be needed.

```
Class:  Ball
Instance variables:  m,  v
Instance methods:
mass:  z
    m := z
mass
    ^ m
velocity:  z
    v := z
velocity
    ^ v
momentum:  z
    v := z / m
momentum
    ^ m * v
```

Methods of Ball

The first method, **mass:**, takes one parameter, **z**. The parameter is assigned to the instance variable **m**. The second, **mass**, returns the value of **m**; the caret is the return statement. The next two methods act similarly for velocity.

The last two methods, **momentum:** and **momentum**, define the interface for setting and retrieving the value of the momentum of the ball.

However, there is no variable which contains the momentum. In **momentum**, the value is calculated and returned. Setting the momentum in **momentum** requires calculating either the velocity from the mass and momentum, or the mass from the velocity and momentum. Since it is reasonable to assume that the mass is fixed (few balls change mass when they move or bounce), the velocity is thus calculated and set.

Note that the protocol for momentum is the same as for mass and velocity. All three values can be retrieved or set. The user does not need to know which values we really keep. All that matters is the external protocol.

The methods provide access to the data without exposing it; at some later time we can always change the access method to do something (even to get the values in a different way), or delete it to deny access.

Using Balls

After defining a **Ball** class, we can use balls in other programs.

In Smalltalk, the name of a class is always written with a leading capital letter which indicates that it is a class. Other variables have a lower-case leading letter.

In this section, we will use the expression **Ball new** to obtain an instance of a ball. For now, consider that this is some kind of magic; later we will look at it further.

In the first group of lines:

```
1  b := Ball new.
2  b mass: 10.
3  b velocity: 38.
```

1) a new ball is created,

2) its mass is set to 10, and

3) its velocity is set to 38.

In the next group:

```
4  c := Ball new.
5  c mass: (b mass).
6  c velocity: ((b velocity) / 2)
```

4) another ball is created,

5) its mass is set to the mass of the first ball, and

6) its velocity is set to half of the velocity of the first ball.

The picture on the right illustrates the new instances and their class.

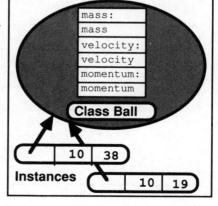

Tracing example lines 1 to 3

Let's examine each line, and the methods that are invoked by each message sent.

```
1 | b := Ball new.
```

The message **new** is sent to the class **Ball**. The value returned, an instance of **Ball** with variables not set, is assigned to the variable **b**.

```
2 | b mass: 10.
```

The message **mass:** is sent to the instance of **Ball** in the variable **b**; the number **10** is passed as a parameter. The message invokes this method:

```
mass: z
   m := z
```

The parameter **z** contains the value **10**. It is assigned to the instance variable **m**. The method terminates and returns to the sending statement.

```
3 | b velocity: 38.
```

The message **velocity:** is sent to the instance of **Ball** in the variable **b**; the number **38** is passed as a parameter. The message invokes this method:

```
velocity: z
   v := z
```

The parameter **z** contains the value **38**. It is assigned to the instance variable **v**. The method terminates and returns to the sending statement.

Tracing example lines 4 to 6

```
4 | c := Ball new.
```

The message **new** is sent to the class **Ball**. The value returned, an instance of **Ball** with variables not set, is assigned to the variable **c**.

```
5 | c mass: (b mass).
```

The message **mass** is sent to the instance of **Ball** contained in the variable **b**. The message invokes this method:

```
mass
   ^ m
```

The value in the instance variable **m**, **10**, is returned to the invoking method.

Then the message **mass:** is sent to the instance of **Ball** in the variable **c**; the number **10** is passed as a parameter. The message invokes this method:

```
mass: z
    m := z
```

The parameter **z** contains the value **10**. It is assigned to the instance variable **m**. The method terminates and returns to the sending statement.

```
6 | c velocity: ((b velocity) / 2)
```

First the **velocity** message is sent to the instance of **Ball** in the variable **b**; this method is invoked:

```
velocity
    ^ v
```

The value of the instance variable **v**, **38**, is returned.
Then this returned value, **38**, is divided by **2**, producing **19**.
The message **velocity:** is sent to the instance of **Ball** in the variable **c**, passing the **19**, and invoking this method:

```
velocity: z
    v := z
```

The value in the parameter **z**, **19**, is assigned to the instance variable **v**. The method terminates and returns to the sending statement.

Alternative Ball Class

Since only the names of the methods are exposed to the outside world, it is possible to change the definition in drastic ways.

Assume that after using class **Ball** for an application, we find that most of the references are to momentum, not mass or velocity. The **momentum:** method executes a divide operation and **momentum** executes a multiply. Changing the definition to store momentum directly would eliminate these sometimes expensive operations.

However, introducing a third variable for momentum is undesirable since we would then have to keep all three in synch. Every change to momentum would still have a divide since the value of the velocity would have to be calculated.

We need to redefine **Ball** with two new variables, one for mass and one for momentum. The new methods are on the left in figure *New and Old Versions*; for comparison the prior definition is on the right.

```
Class: Ball                          Class: Ball
Instance variables: ms, mm           Instance variables: m, v
Instance methods:                    Instance methods:
mass: z                              mass: z
    ms := z                              m := z
mass                                 mass
    ^ ms                                 ^ m
velocity: z                          velocity: z
    mm := ms * z                         v := z
velocity                             velocity
    ^ mm / ms                            ^ v
momentum: z                          momentum: z
    mm := z                              v := z / m
momentum                             momentum
    ^ mm                                 ^ m * v
```

New and Old Versions

The left definition is the new version of class **Ball**; the right definition is the previous version.

The definition for mass is the same (except that the instance variable **m** is now **ms**). The momentum is now stored in the instance variable **mm** and simply has to be set and retrieved. The velocity is no longer stored but is calculated as needed.

Although the new definition calculates velocity rather than the momentum, the changes are purely internal and none of the code that uses **Ball** would require any change, unless that code was (somehow) timing dependent.

However, there is an order dependency. A user of the first version must set the mass and velocity of a new ball before setting momentum or momentum will not have valid values to use in the division (z / m). Users of the second version must set mass and momentum first.

This exposure of the internal implementation of the class to its users is highly undesirable. This problem will be addressed in the next section.

Messages to Classes

In Smalltalk we can send messages to classes too. Classes can also have methods.[22] Usually these methods create new instances of the class. The **new** message is simply a system-defined message to a class.

It would be nice to be able to create a ball with mass already set, and velocity set to zero. Otherwise we have potential bugs from uninitialized values, and an order dependency as we saw in the previous section. (Smalltalk does initializes each instance variable, but it is to an "empty" special value called **nil**, not to values useful in balls.)

We might like to write the previous example like this:

```
b := Ball mass: 10.
b velocity: 38.

c := Ball mass: (b mass).
c velocity: ((b velocity) / 2)
```

In the first line, we want to send the **mass:** message to class **Ball** and get back an instance with a mass of 10 and a velocity of 0. This would be a valid ball. We would never have one with invalid variables to make an error with and there would be no order dependency in instance methods.

Class method for Ball

We can write class methods to allow such code to be valid. We write methods for classes in the class definition.

Class methods are methods that are executed by sending messages to the name of the class itself, rather than to an instance of the class. The **new** message is an example of a class message provided in Smalltalk by default.

Class methods look just like instance methods and can have the same names. They are very different since they belong to the class, not the instance.

The class definition for **Ball** would now be:

```
Class: Ball
Class Methods:
mass: z
    | temp |
    (z <= 0) ifTrue: [ (error message & stop) ].
    temp := Ball new.
    temp mass: z.
    temp velocity: 0.
    ^ temp
```

The class method **mass:** is defined. It is run when the **mass:** message is sent to the class **Ball**. (Remember, this is quite a different method than the **mass:** method which belongs to *instances* of **Ball**; that one is run when the **mass:** message is sent to the *instance*.)

The first line of the definition declares the local variable **temp**.

The second checks the value of the parameter, which is to be the mass, to assure that it is valid for a mass. If not, an error message of some kind is issued and the method stops. (The code to issue an error message isn't shown.)

Next, a new instance of **Ball** is created and assigned to **temp**. The next two lines set the mass and velocity. Finally, the new instance is returned.[23]

Class Methods

As we've seen, classes can have their own methods.

However, it can be confusing at first, especially when a class and an instance of that class both have methods with the same name.

Class and instance methods are quite distinct.

Class methods are run by sending messages to the class itself:

```
b := Ball mass: 10.
```

Instance methods are run by sending messages to an instance of a class:

```
b velocity: 20
```

Lets look at the **mass:** methods for instances of **Ball** and for class **Ball** itself in figure *Mass Methods*.

Why do we need a **mass:** method for instances at all? Why can't the **mass:** method in the class simply set the variable **ms**? One reason is that classes cannot directly reference variables in instances. Classes in Smalltalk are really full fledged objects themselves and no object can set the variables of another.

Another reason is that while there is just one class named **Ball**, there may be hundreds or thousands of instances of **Ball**.

Class: **Ball**
Instance Variables: **ms, mm**
Instance Methods:
<u>**mass: z**</u>

```
    ms := z
```
<u>**mass**</u>

```
    ^ ms
```

Class: **Ball**
Class Methods:
<u>**mass: z**</u>

```
    | temp |
    (z <= 0)
        ifTrue: [(err msg)] .
    temp := Ball new.
    temp mass: z.
    temp velocity: 0.
    ^ temp
```

Mass Methods

The left definitions are the instance methods; the right definition is the class method.

Talking about instances

It is common to talk about instances using the name of their class, but with a lower-case leading letter. We refer to instances of class **Ball** as balls, for example, and instances of class **Array** as arrays. This is not a part of the Smalltalk language but just a useful convention.

Self

Methods can only be invoked by sending messages. Within a method of an object it is still necessary to send a message to invoke another method of that object.

Assume we add a new instance method to **Ball** that needs to execute another instance method of **Ball**. The new method cannot send the message to **Ball** since that is the class. Instance methods are invoked by sending messages to instances. But what is the instance on behalf of which a method is running?

Smalltalk has a special name for this object, **self**. Messages sent to **self** invoke instance methods of that same object.

If we wanted to, say, add a comparison operator to class **Ball** so that balls could be compared, we might do it this way:

```
Class: Ball
Instance Methods:
> b
    ^ (self momentum) > (b momentum)
```

First, this defines a method with a special name ">." It is invoked by writing something like:

```
ball1 > ball2
```

which says: send the > message to **ball1** passing **ball2** as an input.

The definition for > compares the momentum of the current object with the momentum of the parameter. The momentum of the current object could be referenced directly (as **mm**), but that assumes that momentum is in a variable. (Remember: It wasn't in our first version and we may again want to change the implementation; certainly we don't want to do things that make it harder to change.)

In the earlier version of **Ball** we could have written the definition of momentum out in full inside of this new method, but that assumes that the definition is stable, and that we are willing to write that definition in more than one place.

However, the definition has already changed once, and might well change again. It is much safer (and easier) to just call the momentum method. The expression **self momentum** does just that and for the same object on behalf of which the > method is executing.

Note that the > in the last line of the method compares two numbers. It is not a re-invocation of this method but compares two numbers.

Sorting balls

Instances of **Ball** now respond to the > message. Since the only constraint on elements of the sort algorithm presented earlier was that they respond to >, we can now sort an array of instances of **Ball**. The sort code does not even need to be recompiled.

Definition of Ball

Class Definition

```
Class:    Ball
Instance Variables:    ms, mm
Class methods:
mass: z
    | temp |
    (z <= 0) ifTrue: [(err msg)] .
    temp := Ball new.
    temp mass: z.
    temp velocity: 0.
    ^ temp
```

Instance Methods

```
Instance Methods:
mass: z
    ms := z
mass
    ^ ms
velocity: z
    mm := ms * z
velocity
    ^ mm / ms
momentum: z
    mm := z
momentum
    ^ mm
> b
    ^ (self momentum) > (b momentum)
```

6

Class Date

In this chapter we will define a class for dates, with variables to hold year, month, and day. In following chapters the definition will be extended to include time.

Dates are common data items in many business programs. Since conventional languages do not define a date type, dates are usually defined as aggregates (arrays or structures) and a set of subroutines to operate on the aggregates.

In Smalltalk, a date can be defined as a class, instances of which hold data for a particular year, month, and day.

The Definition of Date

The definition of class **Date** in this chapter will be small; in a production quality system many more methods would be defined. However, this definition is functional, and the extensions one would have to make are similar to the methods given here.

Dates clearly have to represent the year, month, and day to users. Some users may want day of year too. We have the choice of which we store internally, and which we calculate on demand. Storing year, month, and day has advantages in that it is more familiar to most of us from everyday usage.

The protocol needs to include year, month, day, day of year, relationals (**>**, **<=**, etc.); protocol to set year, month, day, and day of year; and protocol to create new dates.

Class definition and access methods

The figure *Class Date: Access Protocol* contains the definition of the class and the methods to access instance variables.

57

The class **Date** is defined with three instance variables: **yr**, **mn**, and **dy** for year, month, and day. Methods are then defined to return each of these: **year**, **mon**, and **day**. Each method simply returns the appropriate instance variable.

Then a method, **year:mon:day:**, is defined to set the variables. It takes three parameters and sets the instance variables to these values. Additional methods are defined to set each of the instance variables separately.

Note again that providing methods for access to the instance variables is **not** equivalent to allowing direct external access (as in conventional programming languages). We can later change our minds and store year and day of year. The methods which set and return month and day would have to be changed to perform the appropriate conversion calculations, but the code of all users would still work. Although we have provided the effect of direct access to variables, the users of **Date** really are not accessing the data directly.

Methods for relationals

The relational messages will include greater than (**>**), less than or equal (**<=**), less than (**<**), greater than or equal (**>=**), equal (**=**) and not equal (**~=**).

Class: **Date**
Instance variables: **yr, mn, dy**
Instance methods:

<u>**year**</u>
   ^ yr
<u>**mon**</u>
   ^ mn
<u>**day**</u>
   ^ dy
<u>**year: y mon: m day: d**</u>
   yr := y.
   mn := m.
   dy := d
<u>**year: y**</u>
   yr := y
<u>**mon: m**</u>
   mn := m
<u>**day: d**</u>
   dy := d

<u>Class Date: Access Protocol</u>

See the text for a description of these methods.

Method for >

The method > compares two dates for relative magnitude. (See figure *Class Date: Relationals* for the definition.) The method header specifies the binary operator (>) and a single parameter. The body defines what value is returned. The year of the current instance (**yr**) is compared with the year of the parameter **d**, which is a date. Note that the > in this expression compares two integers, not two dates.

The variables **true** and **false** are defined within Smalltalk to hold the two logical values. These are the same results that are returned by relationals. Thus, writing **(2 < 3)** has the same result as writing **true**.

If the test fails, then the inverse test is made. If it fails, the years are equal and the month must be tested. A similar pair of tests returns the answer if the months are not equal. If the months are equal, the result depends on the relationship of the days; the last line

---

Class: **Date**
Instance methods:
> d
```
    yr > (d year)    ifTrue:  [^true].
    yr < (d year)    ifTrue:  [^false].
    mn > (d mon)     ifTrue:  [^true].
    mn < (d mon)     ifTrue:  [^false].
    ^ dy > (d day)
```
<= d
```
    ^ (self > d) not
```
< d
```
    yr < (d year)    ifTrue:  [^true].
    yr > (d year)    ifTrue:  [^false].
    mn < (d mon)     ifTrue:  [^true].
    mn > (d mon)     ifTrue:  [^false].
    ^ dy < (d day)
```
>= d
```
    ^ (self < d) not
```
= d
```
    ^ (yr = (d year)) &
      (mn = (d mon))  &
      (dy = (d day))
```
~= d
```
    ^ (self = d) not
```

Class Date: Relationals

The definitions for the methods which implement the relational messages.

returns **true** if the day in this instance is greater than that of the parameter, and **false** otherwise.

Method for <=

The method for **<=** is defined as the inverse of **>**. The variable **self** contains the date which appeared on the left side of the **<=** operator (that is the instance to which the message **<=** was sent). The message **self > d** compares the same two dates for the opposite relation and returns true or false; the **not** unary message inverts the result.

This coding technique has two benefits: first we only have to code and debug the messy comparison of two dates once, not twice; second we can take advantage of this later when we extend **Date**.

Methods for < >=

The methods for **<** and **>=** are similar to **>** and **<=**.

Methods for = ~=

The test for equality simply tests each element of the two dates for equality. The **&** message in method = returns true of both the object and the input are true.

The method for inequality, **~=**, returns the inverse of equality.

Class methods

The class method **year:mon:day:** (see below) creates a new instance of date (**Date new**) and then sends the **year:mon:day:** message to that instance to set its values. It then returns the resulting new instance to the caller of the class method.

```
Class:   Date
Class methods:
year: y mon: m day: d
   ^(Date new) year: y mon: m day: d
```

In effect, the statement does this:

```
Class:   Date
Class methods:
year: y mon: m day: d
   | temp |
   newDate := Date new.
   temp := newDate year: y mon: m day: d.
   ^ temp
```

(Remember that vertical bars delimit the list of local variables for the method.)

Implicit return values

In Smalltalk, every method returns a value. If there is no explicit return statement, then **self** is returned. The expression above takes advantage of the fact that the instance method **year:mon:day:** returns **self** by default, and returns that value on back to the caller. The instance method is this:

```
Class:   Date
Instance methods:
year: y mon: m day: d
    yr  := y.
    mn  := m.
    dy  := d
```

This is exactly equivalent to this:

```
Class: Date
Instance methods:
year: y mon: m day: d
    yr  := y.
    mn  := m.
    dy  := d.
    ^ self
```

Copying instances

The **copy** method invokes the class method **year:mon:day:** to create a new instance with the same instance variables as the current instance and returns that new instance.

```
Class: Date
Instance methods:
copy
    ^ Date   year: yr   mon: mn   day: dy
```

This method effectively copies an instance by making a new instance and setting the instance variables of the new instance to those of the original.

Copying and Assigning

Assignment does not make a copy of an instance. Assigning one instance variable to another simply causes both to refer to the same object; assignment stores a reference to the object, not the object itself.

Consider the code below where a new instance of **Date** is assigned to **d**, then **d** is assigned to **e** and a copy of **d** is assigned to **f**. Then a message is sent to **e** to change the month.

```
d := Date year: 1990 month: 3 day: 22.
e := d.
f := d copy.

e month: 9.
```

Sending messages to **e** is the same as sending messages to **d** since they are the same object. Thus, the last line changes the month in the instance of date which "is in" both **d** and **e**. However, the instance in **f** is a different instance and is not changed.

Using Date

Lets look at a slightly longer example of the use of dates. First we make two instances of **Date**.

```
b := Date   year: 1941   mon: 12   day: 13.
d := Date   year: 1949   mon: 7    day: 6.
```

Given these instances we might then write:

```
gap := (d year) - (b year).
f := (d copy) year: ((d year) + 1)
```

The first line obtains the years of the two dates and subtracts them, placing the (integer) result into variable **gap**. The second line makes a copy of the instance of **Date** in **d** and changes the year component to be one year later. The new instance then holds the date: **1949, 7, 6**.

Definition of Date

The full definition of **Date** written in this chapter is repeated below.

Class Definition

```
Class:  Date
Instance variables:  yr, mn, dy
```

Class Methods

```
Class: Date
Class methods:
year: y mon: m day: d
    ^ (Date new) year: y mon: m day: d
```

Instance Methods: Access

```
Class: Date
Instance methods:
year
    ^ yr
mon
    ^ mn
day
    ^ dy
year: y mon: m day: d
    yr := y.
    mn := m.
    dy := d
year: y
    yr := y
mon: m
    mn := m
day: d
    dy := d
```

Instance Method: copy

```
Class: Date
Instance methods:
copy
    ^ Date  year: yr  mon: mn  day: dy
```

Instance Methods: > <=

```
Class: Date
Instance methods:
> d
    yr > (d year)  ifTrue: [^true].
    yr < (d year)  ifTrue: [^false].
    mn > (d mon)   ifTrue: [^true].
    mn < (d mon)   ifTrue: [^false].
    ^ dy > (d day)
<= d
    ^ (self > d) not
```

Instance Methods: < >=

```
Class: Date
Instance methods:
< d
   yr < (d year)  ifTrue: [^true].
   yr > (d year)  ifTrue: [^false].
   mn < (d mon)   ifTrue: [^true].
   mn > (d mon)   ifTrue: [^false].
   ^ dy < (d day)
>= d
   ^ (self < d) not
```

Instance Methods: = ~=

```
Class: Date
Instance methods:
= d
   ^ (yr = (d year)) &
     (mn = (d mon))  &
     (dy = (d day))
~= d
   ^ (self = d) not
```

7

Inheritance

To this point, classes have been individual things. They lived separately, like programs in conventional languages, and looked much like them.

Classes are more social than programs, however. They really live in a network of other classes that are related in various ways. Classes have parents, from which they inherit some or most of their identity. Classes have children to which they pass some or much of their identity.

New classes can be defined in terms of existing classes. The new class, the child, needs only to specify what makes it different from the existing class, the parent.

The new class "refers" to the existing class, in effect including the existing definition as the base for the definition of the new class. Changes are then made in three ways:

1) Addition of new variables;

2) Addition of new class or instance methods; and/or

3) Overriding existing methods by writing new methods that replace them.

The new class does not copy the existing definition, but refers to it as a parent class or *superclass*. The new class is called the *subclass*. Existing methods of the parent can be overridden simply by writing a replacement. The overriding method can also refer to the original method, as we'll see in the next chapter.

This chapter defines a **Time** class, based on **Date**. A later chapter describes how such classes live together and refer to common methods.

Extending Date

Having a class that knows all about dates, we have a base on which to build in a number of directions.

One application might work with holidays and need to have objects that represent specific holidays. These objects would need to know the year, month, and day, as well as the name of the holiday and possibly in what countries, or in which religions, the holiday is recognized.

One could define a new object that has year, month, and day variables plus name and countries. In a conventional language we'd probably have to do that.

In an object-oriented language we can make a new class that includes the full definition of **Date**, and adds two new variables and methods to work with them.

We get the full (debugged) definition of **Date** for free. We don't change it, we don't copy it, and we don't debug it again. We only debug those things we add or change.

Alternatively, we might have an application that works with time of day. It might implement a new class that holds only hour, minute, and second, but it also might want days, months, and years. Again, a new class could be written, but it would also be possible to subclass class **Date** and add the variables, hour, minute, and second.

The figure *Date, Time, and Holiday* shows these two possible subclasses of **Date**.

A **Holiday** class has two new instance variables for the name of the holiday and for a list of countries in which the holiday is observed.

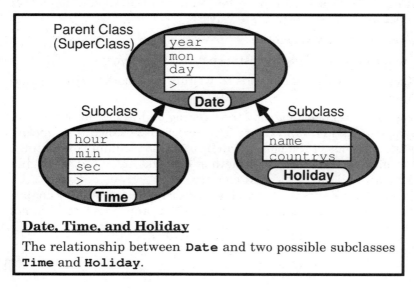

Date, Time, and Holiday

The relationship between **Date** and two possible subclasses **Time** and **Holiday**.

Instance methods would be defined to set and retrieve these new variables, a class method would be defined to create an instance for a specific holiday, and an instance method defined to ask if a given date was that holiday.

A **Time** class has additional instance variables for hour, minute, and second, has methods to set and retrieve these new values, and has new definitions for comparisons (since there are more variables to compare).

In both cases the new class would depend on the existing **Date** class for much of its definition; some methods would be shared between the definitions, and all instance variables of the parent class would be instance variables of the subclass.

Extending Date: Time

This section defines a **Time** class based on the previous definition of **Date**.

The following tables show what parts of **Date** will be inherited and what new things will need to be defined. The **Date** column shows the variables and methods defined for class **Date**; the **Time** column shows those that will be inherited, overridden, or added for class **Time**.

Variables

Date	Time
yr, mn, dy	(inherited) hr, min, sc

Instance Methods: Access

Date	Time
year, mon, day year:mon:day: year:, mon:, day:	(inherited) year:mon:day: (inherited) year:mon:day:hour:min:sec: hour: min: sec: hour min sec

Instance Methods: Other

Date	Time
`<=`	(inherited)
`>`	`>`
`<`	`<`
`=`	`=`
`~=`	(inherited)
`copy`	`copy`

Class Methods

Date	Time
`year:mon:day:`	`year:mon:day:` `year:mon:day:hour:min:sec:`

Relationship between Date and Time

Class **Date** remains a full-fledged class; its users are unaware that it has been subclassed. Class **Time** is a full-fledged class too; its users are unaware that it has been defined by subclassing. Each can have instances, as shown in the figure *Date and Time with Instances*.

Messages to subclasses

Since not all of the methods of a class are in the class, but can be in

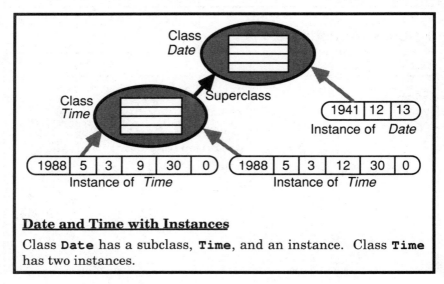

Date and Time with Instances

Class **Date** has a subclass, **Time**, and an instance. Class **Time** has two instances.

the parent, a message send now has to look in the superclass for some methods. Method lookup proceeds like this:

1) Look in the subclass for the method;

2) If absent, look in the superclass;

3) If absent, look in that class's superclass;

and so on. Only if a scan of all superclasses fails to find a method is it determined to be missing.

For example, the > message to an instance of **Time** would find the method in **Time** where it would be implemented. However the message **year** to an instance of **Time** would find the method in **Date**, since it is redefined in **Time**.

Access methods

The first thing to define is the class, the new instance variables, and the methods that will access the new instance variables. (See figure *Class Time: Access Methods*.)

The class **Time** is defined as a subclass of **Date**. Additional instance variables are listed. Since **Time** is a subclass of **Date**, the instance variables of **Date** are a part of the definition of **Time** and need not be specified again.

Methods are then defined for retrieving and setting the new instance variables.

Next, a method is defined for setting all the instance variables at one time. We'll use this when we create new instances.

```
Class:      Time
SuperClass: Date
Instance Variables:   hr, min, sc
Instance Methods:
hour
     ^ hr
min
     ^ min
sec
     ^ sc
hour: h
    hr   := h
min: x
    min := x
sec: s
    sc   := s
```

Class Time: Access Methods

The definition of the access methods for class **Time**.

```
Class: Time
Instance Methods:
year: y  mon: m  day: d  hour: h  min: x  sec: s
    yr  := y.
    mn  := m.
    dy  := d.
    hr  := h.
    min := x.
    sc  := s
```

Time class methods

One new class method will be defined; it will create a new instance of **Time** and fill in all its variables.

```
Class: Time
Class Methods:
year: y  mon: m  day: d  hour: h  min: x  sec: s
    ^(Time new)
        year: y   mon: m   day: d
        hour: h   min: x   sec: s
```

(Note that the **year:mon:day:hour:min:sec:** message is written across two lines. Smalltalk allows writing messages and statements across as many lines as one wishes; a period always separates one statement from the next.)

In a manner similar to the **year:mon:day:** method of **Date**, a new instance of **Time** is obtained and all its instance variables are set.

Overriding

There is a problem though. If the **year:mon:day:** method of **Date** is inherited by **Time**, it won't set the new variables. Thus if the **year:mon:day:** message was sent to **Time**, the instance returned would not have properly initialized instance variables.

The following class method in **Time** corrects this problem by forcing the values to zero.

```
Class: Time
Class Methods:
year: y  mon: m  day: d
    ^(Time new)
        year: y   mon: m   day: d
        hour: 0   min: 0   sec: 0
```

A similar problem exists with the instance method of the same name. It, too, must be reimplemented so that it sets hour, minute, and second to zero.

```
Class: Time
Instance Methods:
year: y mon: m day: d
    yr   := y.
    mn   := m.
    dy   := d.
    hr   := 0.
    min  := 0.
    sc   := 0
```

Using Time

Class **Time** can be used just like the previous **Date** example by simply changing the name of the class.

```
b := Time   year: 1941   mon: 12   day: 13.
d := Time   year: 1949   mon: 7    day: 6.
```

Given these instances we might then write, as before:

```
gap := (d year) - (b year).
f := (d copy) year: ((d year) + 1)
```

Although this does work, it of course does not utilize the full capabilities of instances of **Time**.

In the next example, a fragment of a larger method, a new instance of **Time** is assigned to the variable **flight**. Then, the contents of **flightLate** (a variable defined elsewhere in the method) is tested; if true, the hour of **flight** is incremented by one.

```
flight := Time year: 1988 mon: 12 day: 2
               hour: 14    min: 30 sec:  0.
flightLate
  ifTrue: [
    flight hour: ((flight hour) + 1) ]
```

Definition of Time

The definition of class **Time** is repeated below. Additional methods will be defined in Chapter 9.

Class Definition

```
Class: Time
SuperClass:    Date
Instance Variables:    hr, min, sc
```

Class Methods

```
Class: Time
Class Methods:
year: y mon: m day: d hour: h min: x sec: s
   ^ (Time new)
        year: y   mon: m   day: d
        hour: h   min: x   sec: s
year: y   mon: m   day: d
   ^ (Time new)
        year: y   mon: m   day: d
        hour: 0   min: 0   sec: 0
```

Instance Methods: Access

```
Class: Time
Instance Methods:
hour
   ^ hr
min
   ^ mn
sec
   ^ sc
hour: h
   hr  := h
min: mn
   min := mn
sec: s
   sc  := s
```

Instance Methods: Set Multiple

```
Class:  Time
Instance Methods:
year: y mon: m day: d
   yr  := y.         hr  := 0.
   mn  := m.         min := 0.
   dy  := d.         sc  := 0
year: y mon: m day: d hour: h min: x sec: s
   yr  := y.         hr  := h.
   mn  := m.         min := x.
   dy  := d.         sc  := s
```

8

Inherited Methods

As we saw in the previous chapter, methods that are inherited from a parent class can be executed by the child class as if they were the child's methods.

Further, the child can replace a parent's method with one of the same name; the replacement method is executed instead of the one belonging to the parent.

There are more possibilities. One might want to extend a method of a parent by "wrapping" some code around it: writing a new method and calling the method of the parent at a selected place.

Clearly, we can do this if the new method in the child has a different name, but it will be useful to do this and use the same method name.

In this chapter we will look at how messages are sent and how messages can be directed to a method implemented by a parent class.

Searching for Methods

Methods must be found before they can be executed. When we were working with just one class, there was just one method with a given name. With inheritance, we can have multiple methods with the same name.

The technique for finding the proper class and method to execute then becomes important.

There are two steps to finding a method to run:

1) Determining which class to start with, and

2) Finding the method within that class or its parents.

The class to start with is usually the class of the instance to which a message is sent; but we'll see an exception later in this chapter.

Once a starting class has been found, the search for a method looks in that class. If not found, it looks in the parent, and its parent, etc. until there are no more parents. At that point, there is an error. We'll not worry about this error here, leaving it to the debugger to report and programmers to fix, since it represents a simple coding error.

About This Chapter

This chapter describes how inheritance works and how methods are found under inheritance. Contrived examples show a number of different cases. In each example there is a single expression which is executed to start the code running:

```
m := aBottom mass.
```

This sends the **mass** message to an instance of class **Bottom** which is held in the variable **aBottom**. The class **Bottom** is always the child class (hence its name). There is always a class **Top** which is the parent class.

Implicit Invocation

Inherited methods can be invoked implicitly by sending the name of a parent method to a child instance, as was done in the previous chapter.

Simple

In the box in the figure to the right, the **mass** message is sent to an instance of class **Bottom** in variable **aBottom**. The picture shows the relationship between the classes and which class has which methods.

When the message is sent, **Bottom** has no method for **mass**, so the parent is examined. It does have a **mass** method, and it is executed.

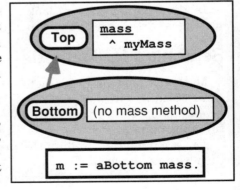

Implicit invocation with self

In the figure at the right the same message is sent. The method **mass** is defined in **Bottom**. It, in turn, invokes method **getMass** by sending a message to **self**; since there is no **getMass** in **Bottom**, the definition in **Top** is invoked.

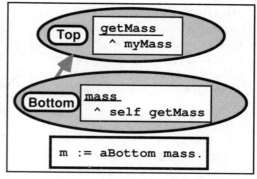

Super

Inherited methods can also be invoked explicitly. Explicit invocation is quite useful when a child class has a method with the same name as that of a parent class method.

The special name **self** is used to refer to the current object, and through it to methods defined in the class of **self** (or inherited from a parent).

Smalltalk defines another name for the current object, **super**, which has slightly different characteristics than **self**. Messages to **super** are to the current object, but the search for the method starts in the superclass of the method being executed. That is, a message to **super** in a method of **Time** would look for the method to execute starting with **Date**, not with **Time**.

As complex as this sounds at first, it is both simple to use and powerful.

Messages to super

In the following picture, the **mass** message is sent to an instance of **Bottom** in which there is a method named **mass**. It is executed. Within it a **mass** message is sent to **super**.

If the **mass** message had been sent to **self**, the search for which method to run would start with the class of the current instance, **Bottom**. However, with **super** the search works differently; it starts searching in the parent of the class in which the message is sent to **super**.

The parent is class `Top` and has a **mass** method too; it is thus executed.

In effect, class `Bottom` adds to the definition of the concept "mass" without changing the concept as defined in the parent, and without having to know how it is implemented in the parent.

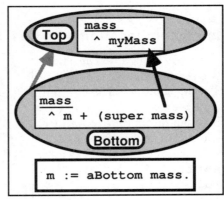

Overriding inheritance

Just because methods are defined in a parent class does not mean that the child class must use them. The figure at the right shows class `Bottom` with **mass** and **volume** methods which make no reference to methods of the same name in the parent. **Mass** sends the message **volume** to `self`. Since `self` is a `Bottom`, the search starts in `Bottom`.

While there is no benefit from inheritance here, there is no problem either; the child can redefine methods as needed. (Some would say that frequent overriding of inherited methods in this manner is an indication that inheritance should not have been used.)

Pathological super

The figure below shows a case identical to the previous one, except that **super** is used in `Bottom` to invoke **volume**, rather than using **self**. The result is bizarre, but legal. The method executed is found in the parent since **super** forces the search for the method to begin there. As a result, the locally defined **volume** method is not executed.

This is not a conventional way to code, and would be seen by many as completely wrong. In general, **super** should only be used within some method to invoke a method with the same name in the parent. Any other use is normally avoided.

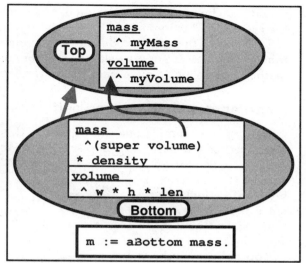

Inherited self

In the figure below, **mass** is again sent to an instance of **Bottom**. There is no **mass** method in **Bottom** but one is found in **Top**.

Within **mass**, the **volume** message is sent to **self**. Both **Bottom** and **Top** implement **volume** methods; the question is which is invoked?

Messages to **self** go to the instance that **self** represents, an instance of **Bottom** here. Thus the search for **volume** must begin in class **Bottom**. Since it has a **volume** method it is the one invoked.

This particular use of **self** provides much of the code sharing power of inheritance. The parent method does not change, but is in effect tailored to fit the situation into which it is inherited.

(The many "application frameworks" available for OOP languages use this mechanism for extensions to the framework.)

In conventional languages a case statement would be used to switch between different ways of calculating the volume. The code would thus have in it each variation, and would be very specialized to the cases it had to implement.

In this case the parent code knows nothing of the special cases that inherit from it. It simply asks for the volume. Inheritance and the method lookup mechanism find the appropriate definition.

Inheritance with super and self

Taking the example one more step, in this version **Bottom** has a **mass** method which invokes **super** to get at the inherited definition.

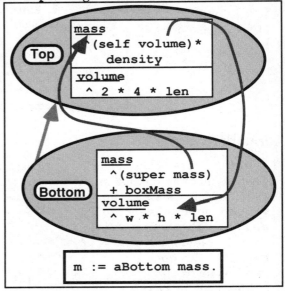

This looks complicated. It isn't as complex as it looks, and since it is a very common situation, it is worth looking at closely.

Top defines methods which are both overridden by **Bottom**. The **mass** method in **Bottom** extends the definition of **Top**. The definition of **mass** in **Top** sends the **volume** message to **self**. Since **self** is an instance of **Bottom**, the search starts there and finds the **volume** method in **Bottom**.

The figure *Tracing Execution with super and self* shows all of the code executed. Arrows point from message send to the method invoked by that send.

Summary

Methods inherited from parent classes can be invoked in a number of ways. In addition, methods in a class can be invoked by calls made in parent classes.

Implicit invocation

A message is sent to a class which does not implement it but a parent does.

The method is found in the parent and is executed.

Invocation of parents' methods

Messages sent to **super** always run methods in some parent (or

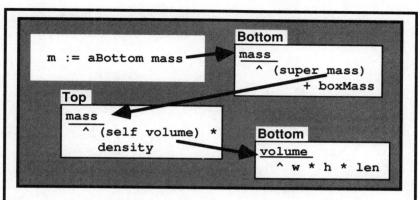

Tracing Execution with super and self

(1) The **mass** message is sent to **aBottom** (top left box).

(2) The **mass** method in **Bottom** is invoked. Within it, the **mass** message is sent to **super**; the search for the method to run starts in **Top**.

(3) A **mass** method is found in **Top** and is run. It sends **volume** to **self**.

(4) Since **self** is a **Bottom**, the lookup for methods starts with **Bottom**, and the **volume** method in **Bottom** is found.

are in error if no such method exists).

Invocation of methods from a parent

A method in a parent can invoke methods in a child class any time it sends messages to **self**, since the search for the method always starts with the object, and not at the level of the method being run.

There are two steps in finding a method:

1) The correct starting class must be found. Except for messages to **super** it is always the class of the instance to which the message is sent. When sent to **super**, the search starts in the parent of the class containing the method doing the send.

2) The method is found by searching the starting class, then its parents, etc.

9

Using Inheritance

Inheritance is a useful and powerful tool. In the previous chapter we saw some of the mechanisms surrounding message sending and inheritance. In this chapter we will add to the definition of **Time** and take advantage of inheritance.

Using Super

Access Methods

The **year:mon:day:** method in **Date** does not know about the instance variables **hr**, **min**, and **sc** in **Time**. If it is used to set the year, month, and day then the hour, minute, and second are not set; this leaves them not set or set to old values.

As a result, we wrote a **year:mon:day:** method to set the new instance variables. (See box at right.)

However, the method with the same name in the superclass already sets **yr**, **mn**, and **dy**. That method can be invoked using **super**.

```
Class: Time
Instance Methods:
year: y  mon: m  day: d
    yr   := y.
    mn   := m.
    dy   := d.
    hr   := 0.
    min  := 0.
    sc   := 0
```

The **year:mon:day:** instance method of **Date** is redefined in class **Time**; it invokes the method with the same name in **Date** to set the year, month, and day, and then sets the hour, minute, and second to zero. (See box at right).

```
Class: Time
Instance Methods:
year: y  mon: m   day: d
    super year: y
        mon: m day: d.
    hr   := 0.
    min := 0.
    sc   := 0
```

The advantage of using **super** here is to isolate the method in **Time** from the implementation in **Date**, not so much to save writing the three lines since the replacement is about as long.

Design of Methods

It is considered good design to try to isolate methods in a class from changes in other methods, and methods in subclasses from changes in a method in a parent class.

Referencing the parent method instead of copying the definition is one example of such isolation.

Referencing another method in the same class instead of copying the code is another, even though the code in the method is very short. (Remember that we used **self momentum** in the > method of class **Ball** instead of copying the definition.)

```
Class:  Date
Instance Methods:
> d
    yr > (d year)   ifTrue: [^true].
    yr < (d year)   ifTrue: [^false].
    mn > (d mon)    ifTrue: [^true].
    mn < (d mon)    ifTrue: [^false].
    ^ dy > (d day)
```

```
Class:  Time
Superclass:  Date
Instance Methods:
> d
    (super > d)     ifTrue: [^true].
    hr  > (d hour)  ifTrue: [^true].
    hr  < (d hour)  ifTrue: [^false].
    min > (d min)   ifTrue: [^true].
    min < (d min)   ifTrue: [^false].
    ^ sc > (d sec)
```

Definition of >

The definition of > in both class **Date** and its subclass **Time** is shown. The version in **Time** uses **super** to invoke the one in **Date**.

Referencing variables in the parent by way of access methods, even though one can access the variable directly, is another example.

Relationals

The definition of > in **Date** is long; it would be useful to be able to take advantage of it when defining a > method for **Time**.

Sending messages to **super** lets us do that. (See the definitions of > in figure *Definition of >*.)

The definition sends the > message to **super**; the method for > is found in the definition of **Date** and that method is run. It returns a **true** or **false**. If **true**, we have the answer and a **true** is returned. If not, then the **Time** instance variables must be compared.

In a similar way we do < and =. (See the definitions of < in the figure *Definition of < and =*.)

This use of **super** has two benefits. First we don't have to

---

```
Class: Date
Instance Methods:
< d
    yr < (d year)   ifTrue: [^true].
    yr > (d year)   ifTrue: [^false].
    mn < (d mon)    ifTrue: [^true].
    mn > (d mon)    ifTrue: [^false].
    ^ dy < (d day)
= d
    (yr = (d year)) &
    (mn = (d mon))  &
    (dy = (d day))
```

```
Class: Time
Superclass: Date
Instance Methods:
< d
    (super < d)     ifTrue: [^true].
    hr < (d hour)   ifTrue: [^true].
    hr > (d hour)   ifTrue: [^false].
    min < (d min)   ifTrue: [^true].
    min > (d min)   ifTrue: [^false].
    ^ sc < (d sec)
= d
    (super = d)     ifTrue: [^true].
    ^ (hr  = (d hour)) &
      (min = (d min))  &
      (sc  = (d sec))
```

Definition of < and =

The definitions of < and = for classes **Date** and **Time**.

reimplement the code contained in the superclass. But more important the code in the superclass can change, say to fix a bug or implement a faster algorithm, and our new code requires no changes.

Inheritance and Self

The definitions of **<=**, **>=**, and **~=** contained in **Date** just happen to work for **Time**. This is not accidental since the original definition (see box at right) had inheritance in mind.

The **self** in these definitions refers to the object on behalf of which the method is being executed, an instance of **Date** originally.

However, when a **<=** message is sent to an instance of **Time**, then **self** refers to that instance of **Time**. The search for a **<=** method thus starts in

Class: **Date**
Instance Methods:
<u>**<= d**</u>
        ^ (self > d) not
<u>**>= d**</u>
        ^ (self < d) not
<u>**~= d**</u>
        ^ (self = d) not

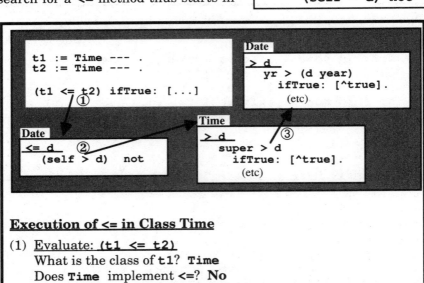

Execution of <= in Class Time

(1) Evaluate: (t1 <= t2)
    What is the class of **t1**? **Time**
    Does **Time** implement <=? **No**
    Does the parent (**Date**) implement <=? **Yes**
    Execute **<=** in **Date**.

(2) Evaluate: (self > d)
    What is the class of **self**? **Time**
    (not **Date** even though the method is in **Date**!)
    Does **Time** implement >? **Yes**
    Execute **>** in **Time**.

(3) Evaluate: super > d
    Does the parent (**Date**) implement >? **Yes**
    Execute **>** in **Date**.

Time but does not find a method there. The search then goes to the parent and finds a method there. It is then executed.

That **<=** method sends the **>** message. The search again starts in **Time**, looking for a **>** method. This definition is found in **Time** and does a full comparison of all variables.

Executing <=

The figure *Execution of <= in Class Time* shows what happens when two instances of **Time**, **t1** and **t2**, are compared with **<=**.

Definition of Time

The following table contains all of the definition of **Time** from this chapter and earlier:

Class Definition

```
Class:  Time
SuperClass:  Date
Instance Variables:  hr, min, sc
```

Class Methods

```
Class:  Time
Class Methods:
year: y mon: m day: d hour: h min: mn sec: s
   ^ (super year: y mon: m day: d)
        hour: h  min: mn  sec: s
```

Instance Methods: Set Multiple

```
Class:  Time
Instance Methods:
year: y  mon: m  day: d
   super year: y mon: m day: d.
   hr  := 0.   min := 0.   sc  := 0
year: y mon: m day: d hour: h min: mn sec: s
   super year: y mon: m day: d.
   hr  := h.   min := mn.  sc  := s
hour: h min: mn sec: s
   hr  := h.
   min := mn.
   sc  := s
```

Instance Methods: Access

```
Class:  Time
Instance Methods:
hour
    ^ hr
min
    ^ min
sec
    ^ sc
hour: h
    hr  := h
min: mn
    min := mn
sec: s
    sc  := s
```

Instance Methods: Relationals

```
Class:  Time
Instance Methods:
> d
    (super > d)      ifTrue: [^true].
    hr  > (d hour)   ifTrue: [^true].
    hr  < (d hour)   ifTrue: [^false].
    min > (d min)    ifTrue: [^true].
    min < (d min)    ifTrue: [^false].
    ^ sc > (d sec)
< d
    (super < d)      ifTrue: [^true].
    hr < (d hour)    ifTrue: [^true].
    hr > (d hour)    ifTrue: [^false].
    min < (d min)    ifTrue: [^true].
    min > (d min)    ifTrue: [^false].
    ^ sc < (d sec)
= d
    (super = d)      ifTrue: [^true].
    ^ (hr  = (d hour)) &
      (min = (d min))  &
      (sc  = (d sec))
```

10

Abstract Classes

Abstract classes are superclasses that are not intended to have instances.

Abstract superclasses are used to define a set of methods, called the protocol, that all subclasses must implement. If the abstract superclass can implement the method directly, then it does so and the code is shared by those subclasses that don't override it.

If it cannot implement a working method, it defines a dummy method that issues an error message. Any attempt to invoke the dummy method gets an error when it runs. It thus forces all implementers of subclasses to reimplement the method.

Abstract superclasses are usually incomplete and any instances that might be made would be useless. They are not a part of OOP languages but are simply a useful convention. In Smalltalk, it is by agreement that programmers do not make instances of such classes. (Sometimes, code is written to assure that instances are not made; it is certainly possible to do so.)

This section discusses several abstract superclasses that are defined in Smalltalk.

Example: Class Magnitude

Objects of subclasses of Smalltalk's class **Magnitude** have some relative ordering. That is, by definition, they will be objects whose instances can be compared. Methods like **>** and **<** should have meaning for all subclasses of **Magnitude**. A partial class tree of **Magnitude** is

Class Name	Abstract?
Magnitude	yes
Character	no
Number	yes
Float	no
Fraction	no
Integer	no

Each of these classes defines objects which have some definition of relative magnitude (i.e., bigger or smaller) and thus each should respond to the <, >, <=, and >= messages.

Characters are values which represent the letters of the alphabet, digits, etc. If stored as ASCII characters (as they usually are), then internally an instance of **Character** has an 8-bit value and the computer's hardware knows how to do the comparisons.

Number is another abstract superclass. Instances of its subclasses can be added, subtracted, have the sine or absolute value taken, etc.

Inheriting from an abstract superclass

Methods can be (and are) defined in **Magnitude** which operate for the whole of its subclasses. For example, the definition of **min:** (see box) works for all subclasses.

The minimum of two values is defined in terms of the < comparison (which must be defined for all subclasses). On the other hand, < itself cannot be defined in **Magnitude** in a meaningful (executable) way since just how a

```
Class: Magnitude
Instance Methods:
min: d
    self < d
        ifTrue:  [^self]
        ifFalse: [^d]
```

comparison is done depends on the exact definition of the data. However, it is necessary to define something so that all subclasses inherit < and are forced to implement it. As a result the definition in **Magnitude** is

```
Class: Magnitude
Instance Methods:
< z
    self implementedBySubclass
```

If invoked, it sends the **implementedBySubclass** message to itself; **implementedBySubclass** issues an error message. (The method **implementedBySubclass** is defined in a superclass of **Magnitude** called **Object**; more on that in a moment.)

Collections

Collections are, well, collections of other objects. An array is a collection and typically the only kind of collection provided by conventional languages.

Smalltalk allows an open-ended set of collections. The class hierarchy (at right) shows most of the collection classes in Smalltalk/V. Abstract classes are italicized. Collections are good examples of the use of hierarchies and of abstract superclasses.

```
Collection
   Bag
      IndexedCollection
      FixedSizedCollection
         Array
         Interval
         String
      OrderedCollection
         SortedCollection
   Set
      Dictionary
```

Collection

All collections must respond to a certain set of messages to qualify as collections. These include:

* adding and removing elements;

* looping through the collection and invoking a user supplied block for each element;

* converting to other kinds of collections;

* returning the number of elements in the collection or the number of elements that match a given element; and

* indicating if the collection contains a given element, or is empty.

Bag

Bags have no keys or indexes or ordering of elements. They act just like a bag or sack into which things are put and from which things can be removed. It is easy, and inexpensive, to ask how many of a given object are in a bag. Bags are useful for tallying things; how many times a given part number was ordered this month, or how many times a given integer occurs in some other collection.

IndexedCollection

IndexedCollection is an abstract class. Its subclasses all have integer keys, like arrays. All indexed collections respond to **at:** and **at:put:** for fetching and setting elements.

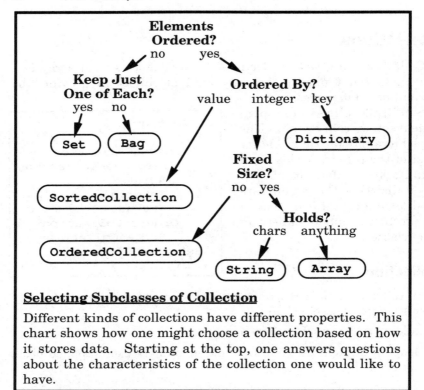

Selecting Subclasses of Collection

Different kinds of collections have different properties. This chart shows how one might choose a collection based on how it stores data. Starting at the top, one answers questions about the characteristics of the collection one would like to have.

FixedSizedCollection

FixedSizedCollection is an indexed collection and an abstract class. Its subclasses have both integer keys and a fixed size. This means that the collection will not grow once it is created. This makes indexing more efficient but the use less flexible.

Array

An **Array** is a fixed sized indexed collection. It can hold any object.

Interval

An **Interval** doesn't hold objects at all. Intervals act like arrays which have been initialized with numbers in a sequence. Intervals are created by writing things like:

```
Interval from: 0 to: 50 by: 5
```

or equivalently, a shorthand form:

```
0 to: 50 by: 5
```

The resulting instance cannot be stored into. It does respond to all other protocol of **Collection** and acts as if it had the contents:

```
0  5  10  15  20  25  30  35  40  45  50
```

String

A **String** is like an array except that the contents of each element must be an instance of **Character**. Attempting to put anything else into an element is an error.

String also has a number of messages for searching and manipulating parts of strings.

OrderedCollection

An **OrderedCollection** is like a queue or stack. It is an indexed collection but not a fixed sized collection. It can have elements added at the front or back (or before or after any element in the collection). Elements can be removed from the front, back, or arbitrarily. It grows to hold whatever is added to it. It can be indexed by integers, just like an array.

Ordered collections are often used instead of arrays because they do grow, and because things can be added and deleted freely.

SortedCollection

A **SortedCollection** acts like an **OrderedCollection** except that it only holds Magnitudes (or objects that respond to the same messages as magnitudes). The collection itself decides where new elements go based on some sorting criteria. By default, elements are ordered with less than (<); that is, any element in the collection is less than all of the elements that follow. The sort criteria may be changed for a given instance to allow any other sorting criteria.

Set

A set acts like a mathematical set: it only holds one of any given object. Attempts to add duplicate elements are ignored.

Dictionary

A dictionary stores pairs of values: a key and a object. The key may be any object but is typically a string.

The Ultimate Abstract Superclass

Smalltalk defines a "primordial" class from which all other classes inherit. It is named (not so strangely) **Object**. It is an abstract superclass and defines a lot of protocol which all objects inherit.

All of **Object**'s methods are real; there are no dummy methods. However, sometimes the implementation is simple-minded. For example, **Object** defines two methods for testing equality (**==** and **=**). The first, **==**, tests that the two objects are the same object. By default the second, **=**, does the same thing but can be overridden by subclasses to perform a more meaningful check for equality, such as comparing the numeric value in subclasses of **Number**.

(In our **Date** example an **=** method was implemented to compare each of the instance variables for equality.)

Object also implements a **copy** method which copies the contents of an instance to a new instance. The one in **Date** overrides this general one but does the same job; we didn't need to write it since we could have inherited it, but ours is probably faster than the general purpose one.

Object also implements another several dozen methods such as:

• What is an object's class?

  anObject class

• Make a human readable string from an object.

  anObject printString

The default is to print the name of the class (**'a Date'** for example). Classes we've written should have provided their own **printString** so that they print a better printed representation of themselves than the class name.

• Is an object of some given class or a subclass? (We'll use this in Chapter 14.)

  anObject isKindOf: Number

• Does an object respond to a given message?

  anObject respondsTo: #mass

(The **#** means that the name behind it is a symbol: the name of a message. Thus **#mass** is the name of the message **mass**.)

• Issue an error message.

  self error: 'I object!'

• The message **self implementedBySubclass** is simply a

method that uses **error**: to inform of the error.

Messages to which all classes respond

Classes, too, have messages that all respond to. These include:

• Make an instance of a given class:

    Ball new

or another instance of the same kind as an instance we have:

    (aBall class) new

• What are the subclasses?

    Collection subclasses

• What is the parent class?

    Collection superClass

• What is the name of the class of a given instance?

    (aDate class) name

Applying OOP

Chapter 11 discusses design in general, then illustrates designing with inheritance with three examples.

Chapter 12 implements the employee pay example from Chapter 11.

Chapter 13 implements the checkbook example from Chapter 11.

Chapter 14 implements latitudes and longitudes in the global position example from Chapter 11.

Applying OOP

11

Designing with Inheritance

Applications in Smalltalk are themselves made up of objects. They must thus be a class, a hierarchy of classes, or some group of classes or hierarchies.

Each conceptual part of an application is itself a class, hierarchy, or both.

Inheritance is used to define hierarchies of definitions of objects, going from the general to the more specific.

The methodology of taking general concepts and expanding them into hierarchies is something of an art, as is all design, but can be illustrated by examples. This chapter will show three examples:

- Employee records: the general concept of employee is specialized to include various kinds of employee and retiree.

- Checkbook and check objects.

- Geography: general concepts of geographic area and position are specialized into specific concepts.

Design Steps

The design process involves three parts:

1) Define a hierarchy of classes, doing the abstractions first and then fleshing out to specific concepts.

2) Define the protocol of the classes: what can you say and how do you say it?

3) Define the state, the data. State comes in two parts:

- visible state, in which the concept is known outside the object. The number of the year in class **Date** is an example.

97

- hidden state, in which the concept is not known outside the object. This is usually information which would have to be calculated if not saved, or which defines the state of other parts of the object. Hidden state is not usually important during the definition of the hierarchy, but only during actual implementation.

Iterative Design

Design is an iterative process. It is rarely done right the first time. It sometimes is done in a different order, depending, often, on what comes to mind first. A simple way to think about design is

1) Do what you know how to do;

2) See if what you just did suggests additional things to do.

Rarely will a design come in a flash, complete and ready and right. It usually requires a lot of thought and preparation and trials before a design begins to feel right.

It is also hard to show iterative design on paper, partly because the volume of detail can be large and partly because each person's steps are different. Thus the illustrations that follow show the result of several iterations. However, they are also not polished examples ready for commercial distribution.

Example 1: Employee Records

Class Hierarchy	Abstract
Employee	yes
PermanentEmployee	yes
SalariedEmployee	no
ExecutiveEmployee	no
CommissionedEmployee	no
PartTimeEmployee	no
Retiree	no
TemporaryEmployee	no

Each employee has certain things in common, including:

- name
- address
- employee identification
- start date
- years of service at last anniversary
- payments so far this year
- marital status
- spouse name

- spouse address (if different)
- birth date
- age at last birthday
- is in medical plan
- medical plan information

However, the way each is paid differs. The class tree above is defined basically on how payment occurs. Each class would have differences. However, all permanent employees would have these in common:

- salary
- division of company
- work address
- work phone (some may not have a work phone)
- manager
- vacation hours accumulated

Commissioned employees would have additional data:

- commission percent
- quota

Executive employees might have this data:

- bonus
- company car

Other Objects

Many of the data items above would probably be other special purpose objects. Medical plan information is probably an instance of some class such as **MedicalPlan**; names and addresses may be instances of special classes, rather than strings; dates are instances of class **Date**; and employee identification number may be an instance of a special class that knows what is a valid identification number and how to form new ones.

All Employees

Protocol for all employees would include access methods for each of the variables. Some allow reading only:

employeeID   set when employee is hired and never changed.

startDate   set when employee is hired and never changed.

yearToDate   Payments to date are calculated internally in the class and are never set from outside.

Other protocol might include:

calcCheck   Perform those calculations that produce a check for payment; return an instance of class **PayCheck**. Update **yearToDate** to reflect new amount paid to employee. (We haven't defined class **PayCheck**, but we'll need one, however it works.)

empType: Change the kind of the employee from, say, **SalariedEmployee** to **Retiree**.

Permanent Employees

Class **PermanentEmployee** contains those things that are common to working employees but not to retirees or temporaries.

In addition to access methods for the additional data (shown earlier), the methods for calculating payment would have to calculate earned vacation. Depending on company policy, this might be so many hours per week or might be done on the anniversary date or at some fixed time of the year. Sick leave time might also be calculated in a similar way.

Note that this code is implemented at the permanent employee level but might be overridden lower in the hierarchy. Part-timers, for example, might have different rules for earned vacation or sick leave.

Salaried Employee

The methods in **SalariedEmployee** should be few. Everything is defined in the abstract class **PermanentEmployee** except those things that make a salaried employee different from a part-time employee or salesperson on commission.

One clear difference is the way that the paycheck is calculated and methods would have to be implemented to perform the calculations properly.

Commonality

Most of that which makes an employee be an employee is common to all or to general classes of employee, not to specific types. As a result, most of the code that would be written for class **Employee** and its subclasses would be in **Employee** itself.

Example 2: Checkbook

A checkbook is an ordinary thing, but representative of a whole class of more complex financial objects. Let's explore how one might make objects to represent a checkbook and the entries in it.

Checkbook Entries

Things that go in a checkbook include entries for checks written, deposits, and withdrawals made from automatic teller machines. Thus we might have three related objects, one for each.

These might be a subclass of an abstract checkbook entry class which contains those things that are common. However, it would seem that a checkbook entry is itself a special case of some more general financial record.

Thus, the following class tree might be used: [24]

```
Object
    FinancialRecord
        CBEntry
            CBCheck
            CBDeposit
            CBWithdrawal
```

At this point we will have only one subclass of **FinancialRecord**, but we can put some code in it and keep it in mind for later when we do some other kind of financial application.

FinancialRecord variables seem to include:

description	A description of the item.
amount	The amount of the item.
date	The date of the item.

Each of these would have access methods.

CBEntry (Checkbook Entry) is the abstract parent class of the checkbook entry classes. It seems to need three variables, which are specific to checkbook entries but not to financial records:

cleared	True when checkbook is balanced and the item is back from bank.
memo	A note about the item.
balance	The balance including this item.

In addition, there needs to be access protocol for **memo** and a way to query **cleared** and **balance**. Setting **cleared** might be by some other method, such as an **itemCleared** method, rather than a **cleared:** method. We may want to prevent anyone setting **cleared** to **false** since once an item has cleared, it is permanently cleared.

In addition, there needs to be some way to calculate the balance given a previous balance.

The **CBCheck** class seems to need one instance variable:

number	The number of the check.

Checkbook Class

The checkbook itself needs two instance variables:

register   The list of check, deposits, and withdrawals.

highCheckNo   The highest check number used so far in the
                  checkbook.

In addition to access protocol, a checkbook needs a way to add and remove transactions, calculate the balance, get the next highest check number, and probably remove items.

Where does Checkbook go?

A checkbook might be a subclass of **Object**:

```
Object
    CheckBook
```

or it could be a subclass of some kind of collection such as **OrderedCollection**:

```
Object
    Collection
        OrderedCollection
            CheckBook
```

If the former, it would have an instance variable (**register** above) which holds a collection. If the latter, the checkbook object itself would *be* the collection.

The advantages of being a collection are that one inherits a lot of protocol, such as looping across all entries, adding, deleting, finding, copying, etc. There is a down side in inheriting a lot of protocol in that one has to think about each method and what it means in the context of the new subclass. If one inherits an **add:after:** method to add something after an existing element, then one has to ask if the checkbook needs to be rebalanced each time the method is invoked. Since it would, then this means overriding each method that adds to the collection. Since collections in Smalltalk are rich in function and have a lot of ways to add new elements, this means a lot of overriding.

The advantages of being a separate subclass of **Object** are that one doesn't have to worry about a lot of inherited protocol. On the other hand, one has to implement a method for adding items to the checkbook, deleting items, etc. For expository purposes, this is a simpler approach, and the one that will be used in a later chapter when we implement the checkbook.

As a rule of thumb, all inherited protocol should apply to the subclass you are creating. If you have to override a lot of methods or (even worse) nullify a lot of methods, you should probably not be subclassing the way you are.

Example 3: Geography

Geographic entities come in two flavors, area and point. Area entities include countries, cities, and airport boundaries. Point entities include lot boundary corner points and survey markers.

All have names to identify what they are.

Thus, a class tree might start with **GeographicEntity** which has one instance variable, **name**.

Under it might be classes which represent areas and points.

```
GeographicEntity
    Location
        SurveyMarker
    AreaEntity
        Country
        County
        City
        Airport
```

The figure *GeographicEntity and its Subclasses* summarizes the classes, whether or not they are abstract, instance variable names, and some instance methods.

Locations have a single variable containing their position. These probably need to be given as a latitude and a longitude, but for now we can simply imagine that somehow the position is just there.

Survey markers have some kind of id number, in addition to a

Class Name	Abstract?	Variable names	Methods
GeographicEntity	yes	name	
Location	no	position	northOf: southOf:
SurveyMarker	no	markerID	
AreaEntity	yes	boundary inEntity	
Country	no		
County	no		
City	no		
Airport	no		

GeographicEntity and its Subclasses

GeographicEntity and its subclasses, instance variable names, and some instance methods.

name, which needs to be remembered.

Area entities have boundaries (by definition). Most areas are within larger areas: cities within counties within states or provinces within countries. Each area would have an instance variable (inEntity) to hold the instance of the area entity that it is in. Thus, an instance of City might have the appropriate instance of County in its inEntity variable.

Positions

Positions on a globe are measured in latitudes and longitudes. If you have ever sailed long distances, flown an aircraft, or spent much time with large scale maps, latitudes and longitudes should be familiar. But in case you've never had the pleasure of meeting latitudes or longitudes before, let's look quickly at what they are.

Longitudes measure the distance around the equator. Since the earth is a sphere, the equator is a circle, and has 360 degrees all the way around. However, longitudes are measured in degrees east or west of an arbitrary line that runs down through England. Since the measurement is both directions, the values are limited to 180 degrees west or east.

Latitudes measure the distance from the equator north (or south) in degrees. A latitude of 30 degrees north means a position that is 30 degrees north of the equator. The north pole is 90 degrees north. Since that is as far north as one can go, latitudes stop at 90.

Any position on a globe can thus be given with a longitude from 0

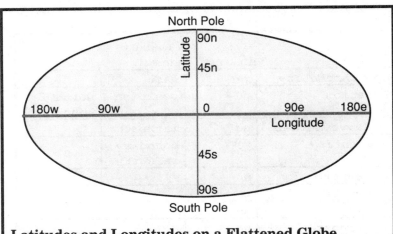

Latitudes and Longitudes on a Flattened Globe

A globe, flattened out so that the whole equator is visible, as are the north and south poles. The directions for latitude and longitude are shown.

to 180 east or west and a latitude 0 to 90 north or south.

Position Characteristics

When designing some new class, one should ask questions about its characteristics.

First, just what is a position? It depends on where the position is being measured. In our case, positions are probably best given as latitudes and longitudes since they are traditional, and useful, ways of placing something on a globe.

* Are latitude and longitude numbers? Yes.
* Can they have any numeric value? No! A latitude of 963 is not valid.
* Can one add a latitude to a longitude? No!
* Can one subtract a latitude from a latitude? Yes.
* Can one compare a longitude to a longitude? Yes.

The conclusion is that latitudes and longitudes are not general numbers but have some of the characteristics of numbers. What operations are valid?

* Latitudes and longitudes with numbers: + –
* Latitudes with latitudes: –
* Longitudes with longitudes : –
* What latitude values are valid? 90 to -90.
* What longitude values are valid? 180 to -180.
* What is the parent class? **Magnitude**?
  (Should latitudes and longitudes respond to >? Yes. Then they are probably magnitudes.)

Why all this work when a number will do the work and we can get on with coding? Simply because numbers do too much and thus don't catch errors such as the following:

* Adding a latitude and a longitude. Any resulting number is meaningless:

  `aLatitude + aLongitude`

* Taking the square root of a latitude. Any resulting number is meaningless:

  `aLatitude sqrt`

* Adding a large number to a latitude or longitude:

  `aLatitude + 43283`

* Dividing (or other operation) with some other numeric type, such

as complex. Any resulting number is meaningless:

```
aLatitude / aComplex
```

Latitudes and Longitudes

Latitudes and longitudes seem to have much in common. They can probably be best represented by being a subclass of some common abstract parent.

Class Name	Abstract	Values	Methods
Object			
Magnitude			
LatOrLong	yes	value	+ - <
Latitude	no		
Longitude	no		

Geographic Position

A position on the globe is made up of one latitude and one longitude. Comparison, other than for equality, does not seem meaningful for such a composite value, so it is probably best simply as a subclass of **Object**.

Class Name	Abstract	Values	Methods
Object			
GeographicPosition	no	lat, long	= ~=

Geographic Boundary

A geographic boundary is some collection of instances of **GeographicPosition**. It could be one of the existing collections, but it seems useful to be able to ask such a collection if it overlaps another or has a simple shape or what its area is; it might also be useful to validate that all the collection members are of the proper class as they are added. (A string is an example of a collection which holds specialized objects; only characters can be put into a string collection.)

Thus, it should be a subclass of **Collection**, but which one? **Collection** has a number of subclasses, some are fixed size, some grow as elements are added at the end, and some allow adding elements anywhere. In the real world, boundaries of cities or countries vary with time, can be refined by adding new boundary points, and are probably most properly modelled by instances with the characteristics of **OrderedCollection**. Since we want to add specialized protocol, our class should be a subclass of `OrderedCollection`.

Class Name	Abstract	Values	Methods
Collection			
IndexedCollection			
OrderedCollection			
GeographicBoundary	no		area overlaps:

Summary of Geographic Classes

These many classes build from simple latitude and longitude to more complex structures. In summary, and in order, the classes are

LatOrLong
The parent class of **Latitude** and **Longitude**, the two parts of a **GeographicPosition**.

GeographicPosition
Defines a position on a globe. It holds two values, one an instance of **Longitude** and one of **Latitude**.

GeographicBoundary
A collection of **GeographicPosition** instances.

GeographicEntity
A named position or area on the globe. Subclasses use either a **GeographicPosition** or **GeographicBoundary**, along with other information, to define the position or area.

Summary

This chapter shows some of the kinds of thought processes that go into designing a new class or a group of classes to perform some job. In each of these cases this process would continue, elaborating the characteristics of classes which represent the things to be modeled.

In Chapter 12 we will examine parts of the **EmployeePay** class further.

In Chapter 13 we will implement the **CheckBook** and checkbook entry classes.

In Chapter 14 we will implement classes **Latitude** and **Longitude**.

Class Name	Abstract	Values	Methods
Object			
Magnitude			
LatOrLong	yes	**value**	**+ - <**
Latitude	no		
Longitude	no		
GeographicPosition	no	**lat, long**	**= ~=**
Collection			
IndexedCollection			
OrderedCollection			
GeographicBoundary	no		**area** **overlaps:**
GeographicEntity	no	**name**	
Location	yes	**position**	**northOf:** **southOf:**
SurveyMarker	yes	**markerID**	
AreaEntity	no	**boundary** **inEntity**	
Country	yes		
County	yes		
City	yes		
Airport	yes		

Summary of Geographic Classes

The geographic classes: the class name with new classes in bold, then whether or not the new class is abstract, then some instance variables of the class, and finally some method names.

12

Employee Pay

In this chapter we will implement a small part of the employee record design of Chapter 11. The implementation will illustrate:

Polymorphism

Polymorphism means, simply, that more than one method has the same name. In a more powerful sense it means taking advantage of multiple methods having the same name by writing a single piece of code that sends the same message to different but related objects. The result is the elimination of conditionals and more compact code.

We will implement only one method in each of five classes, and show how the methods get called through polymorphism.

Hierarchy of Definitions

The kinds of employee, considered by the way they get paid, will form a hierarchy of definitions.

Employee Records

We will implement code for the following subset of the class hierarchy defined earlier. (Class names in italics are abstract classes.)

Class Hierarchy	Abstract
Employee	yes
PermanentEmployee	yes
SalariedEmployee	no
ExecutiveEmployee	no
CommissionedEmployee	no

Defining Employee

Our partial definition of **Employee** is:

```
Class: Employee
SuperClass:   Object
Instance Variables:
Instance Methods:
earns
    self implementedBySubclass
```

Employee is an abstract superclass. Here we specify that all subclasses must implement **earns**.

Defining PermanentEmployee

PermanentEmployee contains no instance variables or methods relating to earning. (It would contain other variables and methods if we implemented it all.)

```
Class:  PermanentEmployee
SuperClass: Employee
Instance Variables:
Instance Methods:
```

Defining SalariedEmployee

SalariedEmployee contains one instance variable to hold the salary, and access methods for salary (not shown). It contains one method to calculate what the employee earns. Here it is simply the salary, so that value is returned.

```
Class:   SalariedEmployee
SuperClass: PermanentEmployee
Instance Variables:  salary
Instance Methods:
earns
    ^ salary
```

Defining ExecutiveEmployee

Executives get bonuses. Thus **ExecutiveEmployee** has a **bonus** instance variable and associated access methods. The **earns** method is changed to include the bonus.

```
Class:   ExecutiveEmployee
SuperClass: SalariedEmployee
Instance Variables: bonus
Instance Methods:
earns
    ^ (super earns) + bonus
```

Note that **earns** refers to the prior definition using **super**, rather than by referring to the **salary** instance variable; this is done so that this method is as isolated from change elsewhere as possible. Next year, all employees could be given a percentage of profits and only the method in **PermanentEmployee** would need to be changed.

Defining CommissionedEmployee

CommissionedEmployee is similar to **ExecutiveEmployee** but with commissions instead of bonuses. Since commissions are typically complex to calculate, we show invoking another method to find the value.

```
Class:   CommissionedEmployee
SuperClass: SalariedEmployee
Instance Variables:
Instance Methods:
earns
    ^ (super earns) + (self commission)
```

Using the Classes

Each employee object is an instance of *one* of these classes. In some class elsewhere, a method might contain this code:

```
e := employee earns
```

This simple message send will send the message **earns** to an instance of any employee type.

Without polymorphism, this would be replaced with a case statement or a sequence of if statements. Then, the next time a new kind of employee was defined, the code would have to be changed to add that new type to the case or if sequence. Since there are many things one does with an employee record, each time a new employee type is added, each place that knows about the kinds of employee has to be found, studied, and (probably) changed.

Polymorphism not only makes code shorter and easier to understand (not to mention potentially faster), but it also eliminates the need for a lot of change later as enhancements add function to code.

Eliminating the exposure of the kinds of employee at each place where something differs depending upon the employee type has a major effect on the maintainability of the resulting code. Changes tend to be more local. Adding a new employee type means adding a new subclass, and at one place in the code adding a statement to make a new instance of that subclass. While the whole system does have to be tested with the new subclass, such testing is much less likely to find bugs since most of the system is not changed.

13

Checkbook

This chapter will implement the checkbook classes designed in an earlier chapter. The example will illustrate:

Inheritance

Checkbook entries will be implemented in a class tree in which inheritance plays an important part.

Polymorphism

There will be three kinds of checkbook entries. Most messages to a checkbook entry will function properly, although differently, because of polymorphism.

Initializing instance variables

A new way of initializing instance variables using inheritance will be used.

Unrelated classes forming application

The checkbook application will have two different class trees working together to form the application.

The class tree designed earlier was for checkbook entries. We'll add a new object, a **CheckBook** class to hold the checkbook entries. The resulting class tree looks like this:

```
Object
    CheckBook
    FinancialRecord
        CBEntry
            CBCheck
            CBDeposit
            CBWithdrawal
```

Checkbook Entries

Checkbook entries are those things that go into a checkbook register: checks, deposits, and withdrawals.

Class FinancialRecord

FinancialRecord is an abstract superclass with one subclass. It exists only because there seems to be some generality that can be split out from the definition of a checkbook entry. Certainly, one can argue for having just one class rather than two. However, having two leaves us with the possibility of reusing some code later. It is always useful to look for generality and to attempt to extract it when defining a class hierarchy.

A FinancialRecord embodies the idea of a transaction with a date, amount, and description. Instances can be obtained and initialized (although we won't). It is not terribly interesting when taken by itself.

Class Definition

```
Class: FinancialRecord
Superclass: Object
Instance Variables: description amount date
```

Class Methods

```
Class: FinancialRecord
Class methods:
new
    ^ (super new) initialize
```

The new method asks the parent (Object) for an instance of FinancialRecord and then sends the initialize message to that new instance.

Instance Methods: Initialization

The initialize method assigns some typical values to the instance variables. The date is set to today's date (using a method available in class Date in Smalltalk systems).

```
Class: FinancialRecord
Instance methods:
initialize
    amount := 0.
    date := Date today.
    description := ''
```

Instance Methods: Access

Both the instance variables and the methods that return those values have the same names (method **amount** returns the value in **amount**); this is not only valid in Smalltalk but is a common coding practice. (After all, if we have a nice name of something, why not use it? Otherwise, as implementers of a class, we have to find two nice names for something and remember that they are connected.)

```
Class: FinancialRecord
Instance methods:
amount
    ^ amount
amount: dollars
    amount := dollars
date
    ^ date
date: aDate
    date := aDate
description
    ^ description
description: aString
    description := aString
```

Class CBEntry

Class **CBEntry** specializes a financial record into a checkbook item.

Class Definition

```
Class: CBEntry
Superclass: FinancialRecord
Instance Variables: cleared memo
```

Class Methods

New instances of checkbook entries are not obtained by sending **new** to a particular subclass of **CBEntry**, but by sending **in:** and passing an instance of the checkbook in which the entry is to be made.

The **in:** method first gets a new instance of **CBCheck**, **CBDeposit**, or **CBWithdrawal** from its parent class (**FinancialRecord**), then adds it to the checkbook, and then returns it.

The **new** method makes it an error to send **new** to **CBEntry** or any subclass. It forces users to

```
Class: CBEntry
Class methods:
in: aCheckBook
    | item |
    item := super new.
    aCheckBook add: item.
    ^ item
new
    self error: '(message)'
```

use **in:** and thus guarantees that all new checkbook entries are in *some* checkbook. (Note how sending **new** to **super** in the **in:** method bypasses this error message in **new**.)

Thus, a new instance is obtained by something like this:

```
CBCheck in: aCheckBook
```

Instance Methods: Access

Not all instance variables in a checkbook entry need full access methods. While it is useful to query and set **memo**, **cleared** should not be modified by anyone arbitrarily. We will just provide a method to query it. It will be set to **true** by **itemCleared** but a check once cleared cannot be accidently uncleared, since there is no method to "unclear" the item.

```
Class: CBEntry
Instance methods:
cleared
    ^ cleared
itemCleared
    cleared := true
memo
    ^ memo
memo: aString
    memo := aString
```

Instance Methods: Initialization

The **initialize** method (see at right) sets the three variables to some useful initial values and then asks the parent class to initialize itself. This assures that everything is initialized properly.

```
Class: CBEntry
Instance methods:
initialize
    cleared := false.
    memo := ''.
    super initialize
```

Note that this method is invoked by the message **initialize** in **new** in class **FinancialRecord**. Let's look at how.

Invoking initialize

First someone sends an **in:** message to, say, **CBCheck**, a subclass of **CBEntry**:

```
CBCheck in: aCheckBook
```

This invokes the code in **CBEntry** (at right).

The **new** message to **super** (third line) invokes the **new** method in **FinancialRecord**. In **new** (see below, right) the message **new** to **super** invokes the system-provided **new** method in **Object** and returns an instance of **CBCheck**.

```
Class: CBEntry
Class method:
in: aCheckBook
    | item |
    item := super new.
    aCheckBook add: item.
    ^ item
```

The **initialize** message is sent to this new instance. Since it is an instance of **C B C h e c k**, it is the **initialize** method in **CBCheck** that is found first.

```
Class: FinancialRecord
Class method:
new
    ^ (super new) initialize
```

Instance Methods: Other

Method **newBalance:** is used to calculate the balance. It takes one input which is the previous balance in a checkbook, performs some calculation to determine the new balance, and returns the new balance.

How this is used will be seen when we implement class **CheckBook**. However, note that we will override this method to perform different calculations, such as for deposits where the amount is added instead of subtracted.

```
Class: CBEntry
Instance methods:
newBalance: prevBalance
    ^ prevBalance - amount.
```

Class CBWithdrawal

A withdrawal is similar to a check in that the checkbook balance goes down, but it has no number as do checks. It so happens that the default actions are sufficient for withdrawals and the definition has no new variables or code.

If the class has no instance variables, no instance methods, and no class methods, why does it exist?

```
Class: CBWithdrawal
Superclass: CBEntry
Instance Variables:
```

It exists because it names a kind of checkbook entry, a withdrawal. While we see no need for code or data today, a withdrawal is certainly not just a negative deposit or a numberless check but a different kind of transaction. Identifying it as such lets the users of our classes worry about concepts and lets us have the freedom to add code later if and as we see a need.

Class CBDeposit

Deposits differ from withdrawals in that the amount of the transaction increases the checkbook balance rather than decreasing it. The only change is in **newBalance:**.

Class Definition: CBDeposit

```
Class: CBDeposit
Superclass: CBEntry
Instance variables:
```

Instance Methods: CBDeposit

```
Class: CBDeposit
Instance methods:
newBalance: prevBalance
    ^ prevBalance + amount.
```

Class CBCheck

Checks have numbers and require protocol to set and retrieve the number. The number needs to be initialized also.

Class Definition: CBCheck

```
Class: CBCheck
Superclass: CBEntry
Instance Variables: number
```

Instance Methods: Access

```
Class: CBCheck
Instance methods:
number
    ^ number
number: n
    number := n
```

Instance Methods: Initialization

```
Class: CBCheck
Instance methods:
initialize
    super initialize.
    number := 0
```

Class Methods: CBCheck

Checks differ from withdrawals in that they have numbers on them. We will assign a new check number as we allocate new checks. Unfortunately for the order of presentation here, it is the checkbook that knows the next check number, not individual checks. Thus we'll have to invoke a method we've not defined yet to get the next check number.

```
Class: CBCheck
Class methods:
in: aCheckBook
    | newCheck num |
    newCheck := super in: aCheckBook.
    num := aCheckBook nextCheckNumber.
    newCheck number: num.
    ^ newCheck
```

First, we send **in:** to **super** to invoke the **in:** method in the parent class to get an instance of ourselves. (Remember, it is in the parent's version of **in:** that we actually send the **new** message which gets the instance.)

We get back a fully initialized instance, since the call to our **initialize** method (the one in **CBCheck**) is done by the **new** method in **FinancialRecord**.

Then we ask the checkbook for the next check number (and put it in **num**), and then tell the new check what its new number is.

We then return the new check.

Check Numbers

Why doesn't the next check come with the next number already set? Because there is no good place to keep the value of the next check.

We could keep it in the class, in a thing we haven't discussed called a class variable. Since class variables are shared by all instances we could have just one checkbook since there would be just one sequence of check numbers.

We can't keep it in instances of **CBCheck** since the next new instance doesn't know about data in a previous instance (or even that that instance exists). Thus we keep it in the checkbook itself, and tell the check its next number.

It would be possible to make a check pad object which has an endless supply of checks. We could then keep the number in the checkbook pad instance that supplied us with checks. This seems to make a simple example more complex than it needs to be.

Checkbooks

We have the objects that go into the checkbook. Now we come to the checkbook itself.

Class CheckBook

The checkbook holds the check register and the highest check written.

Class Definition

```
Class:   CheckBook
SuperClass: Object
Instance variables: register highCheckNo
```

Neither of the instance variables will be exposed directly to users, and there will be no access methods.

Class Methods

```
Class:   CheckBook
Class methods:
new
     ^ (super new) initialize
```

Instance Methods: Initialization

The initialize method of **CheckBook** is called from the class method **new**.

```
Class:   CheckBook
Instance variables: register highCheckNo
Instance Methods:
initialize
    | temp |
    highCheckNo:= 0.
    register := OrderedCollection new.
    temp := CBDeposit in: self.
    temp amount: 0
```

The checkbook register is the place where checkbook entries are kept. It will be an **OrderedCollection**, which can grow as needed.

If we simply set **register** to an empty instance of **OrderedCollection**, then some other code (below) will break. In particular, the code that returns the checkbook balance assumes at least one of something in the checkbook. It is probable that an expanded version of this class would have additional methods that would also break if they failed to check for an empty check register.

To prevent such bugs, we put in an entry, a deposit with a value of zero with these lines:

```
first := CBDeposit in: self.
first amount: 0.
register add: first
```

Instance Methods: Balance

The **balance** method returns the current checkbook balance, which is the balance after the last item has been processed.

An instance of **OrderedCollection** can be asked for the first entry or the last entry in the collection.

Thus, we simply ask the last entry in the register for its balance.

```
Class: CheckBook
Instance methods:
balance
    | bal |
    bal := 0.
    register do: [ :item |
        bal := item newBalance: bal
        ].
    ^ bal
```

Most of this method is a loop which takes the elements of the check register and, one at a time, asks each to calculate the balance. It works like this:

- The variable **register** holds an **OrderedCollection**.

- The **do:** message to **register** causes the block to be invoked once for each element in **register**.

- The block takes one parameter, **item**, which is indicated as a parameter by having a leading colon and by preceding the vertical bar.

- The **newBalance:** message to each item asks it to adjust the value in **bal** and return an updated balance which is assigned back to **bal**.

- When the loop ends the resulting value in **bal** is returned.

Instance Methods: Register

Given a check or other entry, we need to add it to the the checkbook. The first method, **add:**, sends the **add:** message to the register (which is an **OrderedCollection** and knows how to add things to itself).

The last method calculates the new highest check number for this checkbook instance, and returns it to the caller.

```
Class: CheckBook
Instance methods:
add: anItem
    register add: anItem
nextCheckNumber
    highCheckNo:= highCheckNo + 1.
    ^ highCheckNo
```

Checkbook Example

The first step in using a checkbook is to make a new instance of **CheckBook**.

Then we make a deposit by sending **CBDeposit** the `in:` message and passing the checkbook into which the deposit is made.

Once we have money in the checkbook, we can write checks using code that is similar.

```
| cb item bal |
cb := CheckBook new.

item := CBDeposit in: cb.
item amount: 2000.
item description: 'Open the account'.

item := CBCheck in: cb.
item amount: 100.
item description: 'Pay Rent'.
```

Then additional transactions could occur, writing more checks, making withdrawals, and deposits:

```
item := CBCheck in: cb.
item amount:  300.
item description: 'Car Payment'.

item := CBWithdrawal in: cb.
item amount:  100.
item description: 'Teller Machine'.

item := CBDeposit in: cb.
item amount:  500.
item description: 'Tax Refund'.

item := CBCheck in: cb.
item amount:  150.
item description: 'Fix Car'.
```

At any point the current checkbook balance can be found:

```
bal := cb balance
```

Summary of Code

Class FinancialRecord

```
Class: FinancialRecord
Superclass: Object
Instance Variables: description amount date
```

Class Methods

```
Class: FinancialRecord
Class methods:
new
    ^ (super new) initialize
```

Instance Methods

```
Class: FinancialRecord
Instance methods:
amount
    ^ amount
amount: dollars
    amount := dollars
date
    ^ date
date: aDate
    date := aDate
description
    ^ description
description: aString
    description := aString
initialize
    amount := 0.
    date := Date today.
    description := ''
```

Class CBEntry

Class Definition

```
Class: CBEntry
Superclass: FinancialRecord
Instance Variables: cleared memo
```

Class Methods

```
Class: CBEntry
Class methods:
in: aCheckBook
    | item |
    item := super new.
    aCheckBook add: item.
    ^ item
new
    self error: '(message)'
```

Instance Methods

```
Class: CBEntry
Instance methods:
cleared
    ^ cleared
initialize
    cleared := false.
    memo := ''.
    super initialize
itemCleared
    cleared := true
memo
    ^ memo
memo: aString
    memo := aString
newBalance: prevBalance
    ^ prevBalance - amount.
```

Class CBDeposit

Class Definition

```
Class: CBDeposit
Superclass: CBEntry
Instance Variables:
```

Instance Methods

```
Class: CBDeposit
Instance methods:
newBalance: prevBalance
    ^ prevBalance + amount.
```

Class CBWithdrawal

Class Definition

```
Class: CBWithdrawal
Superclass: CBEntry
Instance Variables:
```

Class CBCheck

Class Definition

```
Class: CBCheck
Superclass: CBEntry
Instance Variables: number
```

Class Methods

```
Class: CBCheck
Class methods:
in: aCheckBook
    | newCheck num |
    newCheck := super in: aCheckBook.
    num := aCheckBook nextCheckNumber.
    newCheck number: num.
    ^ newCheck
```

Instance Methods

```
Class: CBCheck
Instance methods:
initialize
    super initialize.
    number := 0
number
    ^ number
number: n
    number := n
```

Class CheckBook

Class Definition

```
Class: CheckBook
Superclass: Object
Instance variables: register highCheckNo
```

Class Methods

```
Class: CheckBook
Class methods:
new
    ^ (super new) initialize
```

Instance Methods

```
Class: CheckBook
Instance Methods:
add: anItem
    register add: anItem
balance
    | bal |
    bal := 0.
    register do: [ :item |
       bal := item newBalance: bal
       ].
    ^ bal
initialize
    | temp |
    highCheckNo:= 0.
    register := OrderedCollection new.
    temp := CBDeposit in: self.
    temp amount: 0
nextCheckNumber
    highCheckNo:= highCheckNo + 1.
    ^ highCheckNo
```

Chapter

14

Latitudes and Longitudes

In this chapter we will implement the **LatOrLong** class and the two subclasses **Latitude** and **Longitude** described in an earlier chapter.

The classes are

Class Name	Abstract	Values	Methods
Object			
Magnitude			
LatOrLong	yes	value	+ − < (etc)
Latitude	no		
Longitude	no		

LatOrLong is the parent class, which will hold most of the code. **Latitude** and **Longitude** are subclasses; the code in them will be whatever is necessary to distinguish one from the other.

In addition, we need to do appropriate range and "type" checking.

The **LatOrLong** example will illustrate:

Inheritance

We will use inheritance heavily; in fact almost all of the code for **Latitude** and **Longitude** will be inherited from **LatOrLong**.

Polymorphism

Some messages implemented separately by **Latitude** and **Longitude** have identical names.

Binary Messages

We will implement a number of binary messages for arithmetic and relationals.

Extending an Abstract Class
We will extend the Smalltalk class **Magnitude**.

Using Latitudes and Longitudes

It often is helpful to pretend that an implementation exists and to see how we might want to write using that implementation. Often, the initial design for the interface is changed significantly by a bit of sample coding.

Creation

```
a := Latitude north: 55.     "create latitude"
b := Latitude north: 23.     "create latitude"
c := Longitude west: 123.    "create longitude"
```

This certainly would work, but it feels more natural to write something like:

```
a := 55 north.     "create"
b := 23 north.     "create latitude"
c := 123 west.     "create longitude"
```

Thus, creation of new latitudes and longitudes seems to naturally be messages to numbers.

Arithmetic

```
diff := a - b.     "integer difference"
further := b + 10.     "increment"
```

Incrementing might push the latitude value past its maximum. What should happen? Is it an error? Probably it should wrap just as if a traveller moved that same number of degrees around a globe. Thus **10 south** - **20** should produce the same value as **10 north**. However, in the example implementation in this chapter we will make it an error, simply to keep the code smaller.

Comparison

```
a < b                  "compare latitudes"
a < 20 north           "compare latitudes"
a value < 20           "compare numbers"
a min: b.              "inherit from Magnitude"
```

Things we don't want

```
x := c - a.              "different classes"
z := 91 south            "out of range"
```

Why should **91 north** be invalid when **81 north + 10** should not? Simply because we want to define addition to act as if a traveler were moving around a globe. It never would produce a value of **91 north**. However, writing **91 north** is asking for a position that doesn't exist.

Class Magnitude

Since **LatOrLong** is a subclass of **Magnitude**, it will inherit all of the methods of **Magnitude**. This means that we need to know the protocol of **Magnitude** that we might need to reimplement, and that part we can inherit and have work for us.

Figure *An Implementation of Magnitude* shows the implementation

```
Class: Magnitude
Instance variables:
Instance methods:
< n
    ^ self implementedBySubclass
<= n
    ^ self implementedBySubclass
= n
    ^ self implementedBySubclass
> n
    ^ self implementedBySubclass
>= n
    ^ self implementedBySubclass
between: min and: max
    ^ (min <= self) & (self <= max)
max: n
    (self > n)
        ifTrue:  [^ self]
        ifFalse: [^ n]
min: n
    (self < n)
        ifTrue:  [^ self]
        ifFalse: [^ n]
```

An Implementation of Magnitude

A complete implementation of class **Magnitude** as it might exist in a Smalltalk implementation.

of **Magnitude** as it might exist in some implementation of Smalltalk.

The first five methods are for relational operators. They are implemented as messages to self that produce an error message if ever executed. This forces all who subclass **Magnitude** to implement these methods.

Why aren't they implemented for real? Because they depend on the internal format of the data. Comparing integers works differently from comparing floating point numbers. Thus they are left for code lower in the hierarchy that is specific to a particular kind of data. However, they are implemented as error messages in order to force uniformity of protocol for all subclasses.

Also, note that not equal (~=) is not defined here. It is implemented in class **Object** as the inverse of equal, and is inherited by **Magnitude**.

The last three methods are complete implementations. They work in terms of the relational operators, will be inherited, and will work for all subclasses.

Class LatOrLong

Since **LatOrLong** inherits dummy methods for relational operators from **Magnitude**, we will need to implement the relational operators.

First, how are numbers to be stored? The simplest way is to have positive numbers mean north or west and negative mean south or east. This lets the relational operators simply compare numbers and be independent of whether or not the ultimate class is **Longitude** or **Latitude**.

Class Definition

Class: **LatOrLong**
Instance variables: **value**

Value accessing protocol

In the normal use of latitudes and longitudes we will not need to get at the value too often; but from time to time we will, and internally within the class we will need to get at the values of other instances.

Further, we need to check the value that is being set, and the best place to put this is within the method that sets the value.

The first two methods provide access to the value of the position.

```
Class:   LatOrLong
Instance Methods:
value
    ^ value
value: val
    self checkRange: val.
    value := val
checkRange: val
    self implementedBySubclass
```

Note that we've made a method name and a variable name the same; both are named **value**. There is no conflict in Smalltalk between method and variable names, and it is common to have names of access methods for a variable be the same as the name of the variable.

The **checkRange:** method will validate that a value is within proper range; it will be implemented for each of **Latitude** and **Longitude**. Again, users will not use this method, but other parts of the implementation will.

Relationals

We need to override each of the relational methods in **Magnitude** since those will simply issue error messages. Since we know the format of the data, we can perform a real comparison.

```
Class:   LatOrLong
Instance Methods:
< pos
    ^ value < (pos value)
<= pos
    ^ value <= (pos value)
= pos
    ^ value = (pos value)
> pos
    ^ value > (pos value)
>= pos
    ^ value >= (pos value)
```

It might look like we are defining relationals in terms of themselves. But we aren't. In <, the instance variable **value** is compared with the result of sending **value** to **pos**; this is a numeric comparison, and invokes the < method of the appropriate kind of number.

Class protocol

The only useful class method simply gets a new instance and gives it a value. Again, this will not typically be used by a user, although she could, but by other parts of the implementation. A second method nullifies **new**.

```
Class:  LatOrLong
Class Methods:
new: val
    ^ (super new) value: val
new
    self error: 'new not allowed'
```

Arithmetic protocol

Latitudes and longitudes can have numbers added and subtracted, and two latitudes or longitudes can be subtracted. Other cases are errors, and we want to detect them.

Validation

First, we define a method to check to see if something is a number, and to issue an error message (and stop) if not.

```
Class:  LatOrLong
Instance Methods:
checkNumber: num
    (num isKindOf: Number)
        ifFalse: [ self error: '...' ]
```

Addition

For addition we check to verify that the parameter is really a number. If so, then a new instance of whatever we are is returned with the sum of the values.

```
Class:  LatOrLong
Instance variables: value
Instance Methods:
+ num
    | val |
    self checkNumber: num.
    val := value + num.
    self checkRange: val.
    ^ (self class) new: val
```

Let's look at that last line more closely:

```
    ^ (self class) new: val
```

First **self class** asks what the class is. It will be either **Latitude** or **Longitude**. (Why not **LatOrLong**? Because we will never make instances of it, just its subclasses.) Since the method is inherited by both, we don't know here on behalf of which we are running; hence we ask.

Then a new instance of **Latitude** or **Longitude** is obtained by sending **new:**.

New Instance

Why a new instance? If not, then we'd get results that didn't make sense, like this:

```
a := 20 north.
b :=  a + 10.
```

If the addition did not return a new instance, but instead changed the value of **self**, then both **a** and **b** would be **30 north** and both would refer to the same object.

Why? After execution of the first line, **a** contains a new instance of **Latitude**. If the addition is done by changing the value of the instance variable instead of returning a new instance, then it is the value held by the instance in **a** that is changed to 30. Then we have to return something, and all we have is **self**, so it is that same instance that is returned and assigned to **b**.

Since that is not what we want to have happen, we have to find another solution. The obvious thing is to have **b** hold a new instance with the new value.

Subtraction

```
Class:   LatOrLong
Instance variables: value
Instance Methods:
- num
    | val |
    (num isKindOf: (self class))
      ifTrue: [
          val := value - (num value) ]
      ifFalse: [
          self checkNumber: num.
          val := value - num ].
    self checkRange: val.
    ^ (self class) new: val
```

Subtraction is more complex since we might subtract a latitude from a latitude (or longitude from a longitude) as well as an integer from either.

So, first we see if the input value is an instance of the same class we are. If true, then subtraction is allowed and we ask the instance for its value and then calculate the result.

If false, we then check to see if the input is an instance of **Number**, and if so subtraction is allowed and we calculate a new value.

(Remember that both **checkNumber:** and **checkRange:** stop if they find an error. They do not return to this method.)

Finally, we check the range of the new value, and if valid, we again create a new instance, set the value as its value, and return the new instance.

Relationals revisited

The earlier definitions of relationals worked so long as the two objects were instances of the same subclass of **LatOrLong**, but the result was meaningless if one was a **Latitude** and one a **Longitude**.

The definition in figure *Revised Relationals* adds error checking.

While this works, it makes for more overhead than we had. There is a trick using polymorphism that makes things much shorter and faster.

It involves moving the definitions for relationals down to **Latitude** and **Longitude** themselves so that we know for sure what the class of **self** is. Then the only problem can be that the second value is not of the same class. If we extract the numeric value of the parameter **pos** with the message **latValue** in **Latitude** and **lonValue** in **Longitude**, we can trap values of the wrong kind.

```
Class:   LatOrLong
Instance variables: value
Methods:
checkSame: obj
    (obj isKindOf: (self class))
        ifFalse: [ self error: '...' ]
< pos
    self checkSame: pos.
    ^ value < (pos value)
<= pos
    self checkSame: pos.
    ^ value <= (pos value)
= pos
    self checkSame: pos.
    ^ value = (pos value)
> pos
    self checkSame: pos.
    ^ value > (pos value)
>= pos
    self checkSame: pos.
    ^ value >= (pos value)
```

Revised Relationals

A revised version of the relationals for **LatOrLong**.

```
Class:  Latitude
Methods:
latValue
    ^ value
< pos
    ^ value  < (pos latValue)
<= pos
    ^ value <= (pos latValue)
= pos
    ^ value  = (pos latValue)
> pos
    ^ value  > (pos latValue)
>= pos
    ^ value >= (pos latValue)
```

Final Revised Relationals: Latitude

Another revised version of the relationals for **Latitude**.

Let's look at the code. First, in **LatOrLong** we define methods making both **latValue** and **lonValue** issue error messages:

```
Class:  LatOrLong
Methods:
latValue
    self error: 'Invalid comparison'
lonValue
    self error: 'Invalid comparison'
```

Then in **Latitude** we override **latValue** so that it returns the value instance variable, and we use **latValue** in all relationals to ask for the instance variable. (See figure *Final Revised Relationals: Latitude*.) If **pos** happens to be an instance of **Longitude**, it will not find our overridden method, but will find the one in the parent and an error message will be issued.

In **Longitude** we do the same kind of thing; we override **lonValue** so that it returns the value instance variable, and we use **lonValue** in all relationals to ask for the instance variable. If **pos** happens to be an instance of **Latitude**, it will not find our overridden method, but will find the one in the parent and an error message will be issued. (See figure *Final Revised Relationals: Longitude*.)

The down side of this trick is that we don't as cleanly trap comparisons with, say, numbers; they will get a generic error message from the system when we attempt to send **lonValue** or **latValue** to them stating that the number doesn't understand the message.

Let's look at how this might work. First we create three instances:

```
Class:  Longitude
Methods:
lonValue
     ^ value
< pos
     ^ value  < (pos lonValue)
<= pos
     ^ value <= (pos lonValue)
= pos
     ^ value  = (pos lonValue)
> pos
     ^ value  > (pos lonValue)
>= pos
     ^ value >= (pos lonValue)
```

Final Revised Relationals: Longitude

Another revised version of the relationals for **Longitude**.

```
a := 45 north.
b := 50 north.
x := 30 east
```

If we write **a < b**, the following happens:
The object in **a** is a latitude. The **<** method is invoked. It is:

```
< pos
     ^ value  < (pos latValue)
```

The **latValue** message is sent to the object in **pos**, which is the object in **b**. Since that is also a latitude, this method is found (in **Latitude**).

```
latValue
     ^ value
```

It returns the value of the latitude.

Had we written **a < c**, then this would have happened:

1) The object in **a** is a latitude. The **<** method is invoked. It is

```
< pos
     ^ value  < (pos latValue)
```

2) The **lonValue** message is sent to the object in **pos**, which is the object in **c**. Since that is a longitude, this method is found (inherited from **LatOrLong**):

```
lonValue
     self error: 'Invalid comparison'
```

Longitude and Latitude

The rest of the definition of **Longitude** and **Latitude** is much simpler than that of **LatOrLong**. We've already done almost all the work.

Class Longitude

```
Class:   Longitude
Instance variables:
Instance Methods:
checkRange: val
    ^ (val < -180) | (val > 180)
        ifTrue: [ self error: '...' ]
```

Class Latitude

```
Class:   Latitude
Instance variables:
Instance Methods:
checkRange: val
    ^ (val < -90) | (val > 90)
        ifTrue: [ self error: '...' ]
```

Polymorphism

When **value:** (in **LatOrLong**) sends a **checkRange:** message to **self**, the method lookup mechanism finds the proper version of **checkRange:**.

This is an example of polymorphism in action. Note how it has eliminated an if test. Had we not used polymorphism in **value:**, we would need to check to see if the instance was a **Longitude** or a **Latitude**.

Another place we eliminated a conditional with polymorphism was in the third (the last) implementation of relationals.

In a conventional programming language we would probably not have been able to share the common code as we did here; if we found some tricky way to have the same code work for two kinds of data, then there would also have to have been an if statement.

Additions to Class Number

All that is left now is to create instances, and that is done by adding new instance methods to **Number**. Below is the code in class **Number** for north, south, east, and west.

```
Class:  Number
Instance Methods:
north
     ^ Latitude new: self
south
     ^ Latitude new: self negated
west
     ^ Longitude new: self
east
     ^ Longitude new: self negated
```

Why pass **self** as the value of the number? Because the number is the object to which the message is sent, and in **Number** and its subclasses, that value is what is in **self**.

Why **negated**? (It means to change the sign.) Remember, we decided to store values as signed integers to make comparisons easier to write. Thus values representing south and west are negative.

Example

Let's look at the methods that get invoked by the expression
     23 north.

```
north
     ^ Latitude new: self
```

This invokes **new:** for class **Latitude**, but inherited from **LatOrLong**:

```
new: val
     (self new) value: val
```

A new instance is obtained, then **value:** is used to set the value:

```
value: val
     value := self checkRange: val.
```

It invokes **checkRange:** to validate the range. But which one? What is **self**? Since it is a **Latitude**, then this method is invoked in class **Latitude**:

```
checkRange: val
     (val < -90) | (val > 90)
        ifTrue: [ self error: '...' ].
     ^ val
```

Summary

Have we taken something simple (a few numbers to represent latitude and longitude) and made it hard (three new classes)?

No. We've taken years of potential bugs and fixed them now. We've made things clear. We've isolated the definition and made it appear in one place, rather than scattered all over where latitudes and longitudes are used.

We've made code we can share with others, that embodies the concepts of latitude and longitude, but not the implementation of the internal form of the numbers.

Look back (or below) and note that there is nothing in the code we wrote that says what kind of numbers latitudes and longitudes are. The assumptions are that values are subclasses of **Number**, but nothing else. They can be integer, floating point, decimal, or whatever our future users might need to use.

Summary of Code

LatOrLong

LatOrLong Class Methods

```
Class:   LatOrLong
Instance variables: value
Class Methods:
new: val
    ^ (super new) value: val
new
    self error: 'new not allowed'
```

LatOrLong Instance Methods: Access

```
Class:   LatOrLong
Methods:
value
    ^ value
value: val
    self checkRange: val.
    value := val
checkRange: val
    self implementedBySubclass
```

LatOrLong Instance Methods: Arithmetic

```
Class:   LatOrLong
Instance Methods:
checkNumber: num
    (num isKindOf: Number)
        ifFalse: [ self error: '...' ]
+ num
    | val |
    self checkNumber: num.
    val := value + num.
    self checkRange: val.
    ^ (self class) new: val
- num
    | val |
    (num isKindOf: (self class))
        ifTrue: [
            val := value - (num value) ]
        ifFalse: [
            self checkNumber: num.
            val := value - num ].
    self checkRange: val.
    ^ (self class) new: val
```

LatOrLong Instance Methods: Relationals

```
Class:   LatOrLong
Methods:
latValue
    self error: 'Invalid comparison'
lonValue
    self error: 'Invalid comparison'
```

Longitude

```
Class:   Longitude
Instance variables:
```

Class Longitude: Range

```
Class:   Longitude
Instance Methods:
checkRange: val
    ^ (val < -180) | (val > 180)
        ifTrue: [ self error: '...' ]
```

Class Longitude: Relationals

```
Class:   Longitude
Instance methods:
lonValue
    ^ value
< pos
    ^ value  < (pos lonValue)
<= pos
    ^ value <= (pos lonValue)
= pos
    ^ value  = (pos lonValue)
> pos
    ^ value  > (pos lonValue)
>= pos
    ^ value >= (pos lonValue)
```

Latitude

Class Latitude: Range

```
Class:   Latitude
Instance variables:
Instance Methods:
checkRange: val
    ^ (val < -90) | (val > 90)
        ifTrue: [ self error: '...' ]
```

Class Latitude: Relationals

```
Class:   Latitude
Instance variables:
Instance Methods:
latValue
    ^ value
< pos
    ^ value  < (pos latValue)
<= pos
    ^ value <= (pos latValue)
= pos
    ^ value  = (pos latValue)
> pos
    ^ value  > (pos latValue)
>= pos
    ^ value >= (pos latValue)
```

Class Number

New Instance Methods in Number

Class: **Number**
Instance Methods:
<u>north</u>
   ^ Latitude new: self
<u>south</u>
   ^ Latitude new: self negated
<u>west</u>
   ^ Longitude new: self
<u>east</u>
   ^ Longitude new: self negated

Summary

Chapter 15 summarizes the four basic concepts of object-oriented programming and illustrates each with examples from the material we've covered.

Chapter 16 summarizes some of the benefits of object-oriented programming.

Chapter 17 is a brief guide for those that want more information.

15

Summary of Concepts

There are four basic concepts in object-oriented programming:

* Hierarchy of Definitions (Inheritance),
* Data Hiding,
* Polymorphism, and
* Single Type (A Variable Holds One Thing).

Hierarchy of Definitions

The class hierarchy provides a framework in which to define abstractions of things and to then flesh out the abstractions into objects which model desired characteristics.

Higher levels define abstract concepts, common protocols, and shared code. Lower levels define concrete implementations. It is common to have as much as 80 percent or more of the code in higher levels of the hierarchy.

The hierarchy provides a significant code sharing mechanism, aids in keeping the effect of changes localized, and provides significant design assistance.

Examples

We've seen a number of examples in this book:

Date and Time

The definition of class **Time** was based on the definition of class **Date** and extended the concept to a finer granularity of measurement (i.e., down to second instead of day). The definition of **Date** was not modified at all and no code that used it would have broken.

Magnitude and Number

Class **Magnitude** in Smalltalk defines the general concept of things with ordering. Subclasses must thus implement the relational operators for their instances.

Class **Number** is a subclass of **Magnitude** which adds the idea of arithmetic operators. Subclasses of **Number** have both the concept of magnitude and number.

Employee Pay Records

We defined employee pay records by defining a general idea, then elaborating it for various kinds of employee.

Financial Records

We defined a financial record, subclassed it to define a checkbook entry, and then made subclasses of that for various kinds of entries.

Data Hiding

OOP hides all of the data behind a wall of code which protects it from access.

Access to the data in an object is only through access methods, if available at all. Access methods have the ability to deny access later, or to redefine how such access is done. One might change a variable access to a calculation or a calculation to a variable access. One might want a variable to be read but not set, or only set to certain values, or only set to **true** from **false** but never **false** again.

This control over access is fundamental to OOP, but not exclusive to it and is a feature of some non-OOP languages such as Modula-2. Some hybrid languages have escapes which let outsiders access data within a definition; to the extent such cheating is necessary (or practiced), some benefit of OOP is lost.

Examples

Data hiding is fundamental. Some particular examples we've seen include:

Balls

The data in instances of **Ball** was changed to reflect an improved understanding of how the instances were being used. The second version we developed had totally different variables, but the interface to the objects was the same.

CheckBook
Several of the instance variables of a checkbook are not fully exposed. The cleared variable can be turned on by a user call, and queried, but not turned off. The balance can be queried but not set.

Polymorphism

Polymorphism simply means that there is more than one method in different classes with the same name.

However, as typically used, the methods belong to objects with some relationship to each other. In these cases polymorphism can replace case statements or operator overloading.

Polymorphism can eliminate conditionals (such as if, switch, or case statements in other languages) and lead to more compact code. One should examine each **ifTrue:** to see if it is really necessary or if it can be replaced by polymorphism.

Examples

Not all OOP code uses polymorphism, and not all uses of polymorphism are as powerful as others. Particularly powerful examples are:

Employee Pay Records
Each instance responds to the **earns** message. Each calculates the amount earned differently. Had polymorphism not been used, we would have been forced to use either a compound if statement or a case or switch statement.

Latitudes and Longitudes
All code is inherited except for:

1) a method which checks the valid range of a new value. An inherited method sends a message to **self** to invoke the proper validation method.

2) relationals which are implemented at the bottom of the class tree in order to use polymorphism for error checking and efficiency.

Checkbook Entries
All instances of checkbook entries know how to calculate a new balance, given an old one. How it is done depends on the kind of instance, with the caller neither knowing nor caring.

Single Type

A variable holds just one thing: an object. In effect, OOP separates the idea of the type of the data from the type of the variable. Variables don't have a type; data does (its class).

Since inputs (parameters) to methods are variables, they too can hold anything.

This concept is fundamental to OOP, but is missing in some hybrid languages and is present only as an option in others.

This concept is controversial. Some prefer to stress the concept of dynamic binding.

I consider that the concept of a single type encompasses the concept of dynamic binding, since the language implementation cannot tell what is in a variable until a message is sent to it.

Others prefer to think of variables in Smalltalk as having no type, but instead think of the data as having type. This is a fun distinction to have arguments about, but the effect is the same.

Some languages called object-oriented require that variables be typed, or partly typed, or declared as holding an object of unknown type. Some think of these languages as only partly object-oriented and some as fully object-oriented. The conclusion one draws often depends on ones favorite language.

When it is missing, much of the generality found in languages such as Smalltalk is lost.

Examples

Since Smalltalk doesn't type variables, any use of a variable is an example of this property. However, many uses do not take advantage of the characteristic. Some that do take advantage are:

Sort example
Our first example, the sort algorithm, depended strongly on getting a collection of data that could be any collection type and which could have any element that responded to a comparison.

Collection classes
The subclasses of class **Collection** in Smalltalk all depend on this characteristic. Other than **String**, all can hold anything. An **Array** can have anything as an element, including another collection. Multidimensional arrays in Smalltalk happen only because arrays can have arrays as elements.

Latitudes and Longitudes
The values can be any kind of number (subject to range restrictions).

Numbers

Smalltalk calculations return different kinds of objects depending on the kinds and values of the starting numbers. For example:

Expression	Result Class	Result Value
8 / 4	`Integer`	2
10 / 4	`Fraction`	5 / 2
10.0 / 4	`Float`	2.5
10 * 10	`Integer`	100
10000 ^ 10000	`LargePositiveInteger`	100000000

Since the kind of number returned from an expression depends on the values, Smalltalk in general is highly dependent on *not* typing variables.

However, the benefits are great. Except in floating point, precision is virtually never lost. Integer division results in fractions which express the full value of the original. Calculations that would normally cause an overflow do not, but simply return a larger value. Integers can be thousands of digits long, with memory growing as needed to hold bigger numbers.

Summary

The four basic concepts of object-oriented programming are not just four separate ideas which were stuffed into a new language, but are four integrated ideas that work together.

In some sense there are two concept groups:

1) Data hiding, and

2) Polymorphism + Hierarchy + Single type

While data hiding is a separate concept, the other three intertwine and interrelate and together provide more power than they do separately.

While polymorphism can exist without hierarchy and is useful without it, it provides much of its power only when the multiple names are inherited.

A variable that can hold anything is required for polymorphism since if we know what is in a variable at compile time (or when the code is written) we also can deduce which of the methods is to be run. Thus if we fully type variables (by naming the object that is to go into the variable), we lose the run-time power of polymorphism.

Together these four concepts define a new way to think about programming and spawn a whole new world of ideas and approaches to design and program construction.

Other Definitions

Casual definitions of OOP often include the idea of message sending as fundamental.

Yet it isn't. It is a result of the other ideas. Given polymorphism and a hierarchy it is necessary to find the method to run. Clearly two steps are necessary: find where to start looking, and then following some algorithm, look until the method is found (or the search fails). Thus message sending is a fancy name for binding methods to their calls.

Other casual (and not so casual) definitions of OOP include the idea of class as fundamental. While Smalltalk has classes, as do most OOP languages, it is not fundamental. Any language having the four characteristics would be object-oriented, whether it had classes or not. Hierarchies are fundamental; classes are just one way to implement hierarchies.

Ruler

Now you have a ruler to measure OOP systems with. When you see an advertisement like the one below,

---

Announcing *HyperStarCalc*
The Ultimate Spreadsheet
Complete with Graphical Interface Builder,
HyperMedia, MultiMedia,
and
Now Object-oriented!!!!

---

you know what questions to ask (if, indeed, you have to ask any!).

At a trade show recently, under a huge sign containing the words "Object-oriented," a friend asked the salesperson just what was object-oriented about their program, a new visual language and interface builder. The reply was: "Well, object-oriented means when you change the code in one object it doesn't change in the others."

'Nuff said?

16

Summary of Benefits

The benefits of OOP are a direct result of the characteristics of OOP. I consider the main benefits to be:

Code reuse
Existing code is much more apt to be used again. It is feasible (and practical) to consider writing something once and having it used again and again.

Localization of change
Changes are usually local to a class, or even isolated in a new subclass, rather than spread out across a whole application.

Design assistance
The class hierarchy forces consideration of design before coding.

Extensibility
Language features and user programs look the same. There is not the split between things provided by the language and things provided by users.

Faster development
Although partly a result of the other benefits above, faster development is important enough to be mentioned separately.

Code Reuse

The ability to write code that can be widely and easily reused has been a goal of large numbers of programmers for at least two decades. No significant code reuse has ever been achieved despite this goal.

However, OOP seems to deliver the ability to reuse code. Much of the evidence is anecdotal and transferred informally from person to person.

It includes statements (from a Smalltalk programming shop[25]) that only 25 percent of a new application is new code; the rest is reuse of code written for often quite diverse applications.

It includes an observation of the author involving a large chunk of code that evolved into a particular function with no plan for generalization; later a very small effort generalized the code and it was used again and again. This reuse stemmed from the natural boundaries that OOP places between different objects.

Code reuse in OOP occurs because of data hiding, inheritance, and single type.

Data hiding builds walls around data and its code, making it more isolated from other code.

Inheritance encourages generalizing code first, then making it more specific to the case at hand. The general parts are often reusable, and often account for the bulk of the code written.

When a variable, parameter, or array element can hold anything, there are fewer constraints built into code. It is not unusual for programmers in conventional languages to write sort routines, over and over. We've seen that one sort routine can sort any kind of data (at least in memory), and in Smalltalk no one ever has to write another sort routine.

Localization of Change

Localization of changes occurs because of data hiding and polymorphism. Data hiding isolates code from other code. Polymorphism removes the need for switch statements and other global knowledge of state. Together they effectively limit the ripple effect of change.

Rather than having to change 20 modules, with unknown effects, one changes one object, with the effects being local to the object.

It appears that large programs written in an O-O language are much more maintainable. Again, there is not a 10-year history of major projects written and maintained in an O-O language. We will not know until then how much better "code maintenance" is with OOP.

Example

Imagine a graphics program that performs various operations on a number of graphical objects. It might display, resize, delete, shade, color, rotate, or hide the objects. It might have ovals, rectangles, triangles, lines, text, or general polygons.

Each operation, such as rotate, must know (in a conventional language) each of the kinds of data it might have to operate on.

The rotate procedure, below, is written in a pseudo-language similar to C.

```
procedure rotate ( shape )
   switch on ( kind of shape )
      case oval:   rotateOval(shape);
      case rect:   rotateRect(shape);
      case tri:    rotateTri(shape);
      case line:   rotateLine(shape);
      case text:   rotateText(shape);
      case poly:   rotatePoly(shape);
   end switch;
end rotate;
```

Each kind of shape is listed in the rotate routine, and also in the display routine, the translate (move) routine, the scale routine, and so on. To add a new kind of shape it is necessary to modify each routine that knows of shapes.

In OOP, the line object would know how to rotate itself, since the rotate line code would be a part of the line object. Adding a new kind of shape would require defining the code and data for the object and then just using it. Each place that an object is rotated in other code simply asks the object to do itself, and does not know what kinds of objects there are.

Inheritance is thus used to isolate the new code, and polymorphism is used to talk to the new code with existing methods.

Design Assistance

Inheritance forces thinking about structure at the start of design process; data hiding forces thinking about both data and the operations on it, before thinking about algorithms.

Objects are written as specializations of other objects. Designing a program requires thought about the objects and the abstract concepts or general things of which the objects are specializations; that is, the class hierarchy is one of the first things to design. Thus in OOP the natural place to start is with general concepts and then to specialize them. How this methodology compares to other design methodologies, and what design methodologies are appropriate for OOP, is a matter of current exploration.[26]

The hierarchy of definitions of objects proceeds from the general to the more specific. A general definition serves as a blueprint for the more specific definitions lower in the hierarchy.

Since the first thing written is the structure of the hierarchy of definitions, the programmer is forced to consider the general structure before writing any code. In fact, he cannot write code until the hierarchy is at least partly defined, and it is difficult to write until the hierarchy is well defined. Thus, the programmer is forced to consider structure at the beginning.

While no system ensures proper design (and some people can misuse even a sure thing), inheritance forces examination of design before coding.

Extensibility

Another goal in conventional languages, this time of the language designers, is language extensibility. The desire is to be able to add new statements and data types to languages. If a particular language does not support picture fields or complex numbers, it should be possible to add them. Further, it is desired that the addition be in the same style as similar features already in the language.

Users of conventional languages have been trained by the limits of the technology into thinking that things they implement are somehow different than things built into the languages. While integer and floating point numbers are built into the language, complex numbers often are not. While arrays are built into the language, queues and sets usually are not. While decimal numbers and strings are built into the language, latitudes and longitudes are not.

But programmers use complex numbers, picture fields, queues, sets, and latitudes. And not just these, but hundreds of other kinds of things. Each of these deserves the same level of integration into our languages that the "base" facilities have.

That is, if one writes **a+b** to add two integers, then one should be able to write **a+b** to add two complex numbers instead of **cadd(a,b)**. This goal has not been achieved to any great extent by conventional languages; no procedural language in general use has ever succeeded in allowing the addition of complex new statements, especially control structures such as **repeat** loops.

Smalltalk not only allows such extensions, it is mainly built by such self extensions including looping, conditionals, and collections. The core language is tiny, probably the smallest of any general purpose commercial language; yet the facilities provided are among the richest of any language. Although C++ allows for the addition of new operators, it does not allow extending other parts of the language.

Faster Development

The development cycle in OOP can be shorter since existing code is more apt to be reused, and because changes in specifications often change less of a system (because of localization of change).

The faster development cycle is real. I'm aware of 18 month projects being done in 4 months when done in Smalltalk versus C. Some of the effect is due to the Smalltalk environment, and the ability to immediately fix and rerun. Few other programming systems have quite the same level of integration and power during development as Smalltalk. Some, however, is due to OOP, and the large body of reusable code that lives in the Smalltalk environment.

Summary

We have considered five major benefits of OOP:

Code Reuse

Localization of Change

Design Assistance

Extensibility

Faster Development

The benefits of each of these are real and can be achieved by mere mortals in real life.

However, there is no magic silver bullet[27] which guarantees these benefits or that solves all programming problems. Even if OOP provided a factor of 3 or 4 or 5 in programming improvement, it takes such improvements every few years to keep up with the factor of 2 every 2 years achieved in hardware improvements, or to keep up with applications development backlogs.

17

Where from Here?

If you've read this far you have an exposure to the basic concepts of OOP. Where you go from here depends on you. There are lots of options. Let's look at a few, chosen from far too many to list. (Appendix A has more information on many of these and on many other sources of related information.)

Just the Facts, Ma'am

... as Sergeant Webb said in Dragnet, so we might say here. If you have the concepts you set out to get, and are not going to program using OOP, where you go from here depends on your needs.

Management

If you are involved with management of programming you might want to explore how some projects could try Smalltalk and some others try C++ or an object-oriented Pascal. Regardless of the benefits of OOP, there is a long learning curve, both because the concepts are new and very different, and because the techniques of development for OOP differ.

Appendix A lists some books that address OOP design and system design using OOP.

Curious

If your curiosity has been aroused, you are prime candidates for one of the object-oriented Pascal, C++, or Smalltalk systems that have integrated environments and lots of sample applications. I personally would recommend Smalltalk/V in one of its many forms if you don't own anything, simply because you've come a long way in this book toward becoming a Smalltalk programmer. However, there are some nice C++ and object-oriented Pascal systems around too. Appendix A lists an assortment of these as of early 1991. More are appearing almost monthly.

Pick one and try something small. If it's concepts you're wanting to understand better, a short program is much better than a long one.

More Concepts - Further Reading

If this book has started your OOP engine, there are many more places to get more detailed information.

Appendix A will point you to other books which explore these concepts further.

Hands-On Learning

If you have a need or desire to learn to program in an OOP language, there are a number of good systems on the market at the time I wrote this, and undoubtedly there will be more by the time you read this. Since things are moving rapidly, the best I can do is point to a few systems as places to start.

Learning Smalltalk

Digitalk's Smalltalk/V for MS- or PC-DOS, for the Macintosh, for OS/2 Presentation Manager, or for Microsoft Windows 3 comes with a tutorial and reference manuals and many have learned Smalltalk this way.

If you have access to a 386, larger Macintosh, or a workstation, Smalltalk-80 from ParcPlace is another commercial system of interest.

Learning C++

Many vendors offer C++ systems. Two that are inexpensive are Borland's Turbo C++, and Zortech C++. Microsoft Quick C may offer C++ support by the time you read this.

For the Macintosh, Think C provides a subset of C++ as this is written. Apple and Zortech provide full C++ development systems.

Learning an object-oriented Pascal

While there are no Pascal standards to parallel C++ for C, many vendors have extended the ideas on Apple's Object Pascal.

For the Macintosh, see both Apple's Object Pascal with it's MacApp development library, and Think Pascal.

On the PC, Borland's Turbo Pascal and Microsoft's Quick Pascal offer OOP support.

Tracking the Industry

Conferences

There are a number of conferences with different goals and in different countries.

OOPSLA

The premiere technical conference is ACM's OOPSLA (Object-Oriented Programming Systems, Languages, and Applications). It has been held since 1986 and drew about 2300 people in late 1990. OOPSLA features tutorials, a trade show, technical papers, panel discussions, and demonstrations. It is held in North America in varying locations.

If you belong to ACM, watch for notices in the Communications of the ACM. Notices are usually listed in upcoming events columns in *Byte* and other publications too.

SCOOP

This series of seminars is held several times a year in various parts of the USA. It has tutorials on various aspects of OOP, panels, and a trade show. Watch for advertisements in programmers' magazines like *Dr. Dobb's* and *Programming Languages*.

ECOOP

ECOOP is the European Conference on Object-Oriented Programming. It is usually held in Europe (except for 1990 when it was held jointly with OOPSLA in Ottawa). It is smaller than OOPSLA and traditionally more theoretical in direction. Look for information in the same places as for OOPSLA, above.

Others

Various other trade shows and technical symposiums related to OOP are starting to appear.

Publications

Several publications are dedicated to OOP. They are:

Object, a magazine on object-oriented programming.

The *Journal of Object-Oriented Programming* (JOOP) is a

technical journal which publishes papers and articles on OOP.

The *Hotline on Object-Oriented Programming* (HOOP) is a newsletter listing industry activities.

OOPS Messenger is a publication of the ACM Special Interest Group on Programming Languages (SIGPlan) in conjunction with OOPSLA. It contains articles and papers on OOP.

See Appendix A for information on these publications.

Other publications that frequently contain articles on OOP include *Byte, Dr. Dobb's*, and *Computer Language*. These are all available at newsstands.

Appendices

Appendix A is a guide to books, periodicals, and software that may be useful for further learning.

Appendix B is a discussion of problems in procedural programming.

Appendix C is a glossary of OOP and Smalltalk terms.

Further Information

At one time it was possible to list all OOP material in a short bibliography. That is no longer the case today. The material below was selected based on reputation, content, and personal preference. Inclusion of an item does not mean that it is better than one omitted, nor does omission indicate any negative opinion.

Software

Any attempt to list current software prices, versions, or capabilities in a book is futile. At best one can give some pointers to what exists at the time of publication. Since software tends to be updated once a year or so, and there are many new products, please take this as merely a starting place, not as definitive coverage of the field.

Smalltalk/V. **Digitalk.**
A learning vehicle; also good for real applications. The tutorial section lets you read and interact at the same time. Implementations for MS-DOS 8088/80286/386/486, Macintosh, OS/2 PM, Windows 3.0, and others.

Quick Pascal. **Microsoft.**
Pascal plus OOP for MS-DOS.

Turbo Pascal **Version 5 and later. Borland.**
Pascal plus OOP for MS-DOS.

Turbo C++. **Borland.**
C++ for MS-DOS.

Zortech C++. **Zortech.**
A learning vehicle; also good for real applications. The tutorial

section lets you read and interact at the same time. Implementations for MS-DOS 8088, 80286, and others.

General Books

Budd, Timothy. *An Introduction to Object-Oriented Programming.* **Addison-Wesley, 1991.**
A more advanced introduction to OOP than the book you are holding, and twice as long, it covers the concepts and provides examples in C++, Object Pascal, Smalltalk, and Objective-C. Contains a section on design methodology. A good next step for programmers.

Cox, Brad. *Object-oriented Programming - An Evolutionary Approach.* **Addison-Wesley, 1986.**
Good discussion of what and why of OOP. Good survey of Smalltalk-80, C++, and Ada. Mainly about Objective-C and its use.

Goldberg, Adele and David Robson. *Smalltalk-80: The Language.* **Addison-Wesley, 1989.**
The "Purple Book." This is the standard reference to Smalltalk-80. It is the language definition section from the "Blue Book" (*Smalltalk-80: The Language and Its Implementation*) of 1983 (same authors) repackaged without other material.

Lippman, Stanley. *C++ Primer.* **Addison-Wesley, 1989.**
Good introduction to C++ version 2 with lots of examples. The emphasis here is on the language. In Mullin, below, the emphasis is on design.

Meyer, Bertrand. *Object-oriented Software Construction.* **Prentice Hall, 1988.**
The first 50 pages are a good introduction to problems with software design along with a good introduction to OOP. The author describes it all in the context of Eiffel, his own OOPS. First 50 pages are general and don't cover Eiffel; worth seeking out a copy just to read them. The full book is recommended for advanced readers.

Schmucker, Kurt. *Object-Oriented Programming for the Macintosh.* **Hayden, 1986.**
Short introduction to OOPS; good survey of Object Pascal., MacApp, Smalltalk, Lisa Clascal; short survey of Neon, Exper-CommonLISP, Object Logo, and Objective-C. Lots of sample code in MacApp (Object Pascal), Smalltalk, and Clascal. Lots of real code to read.

Advanced Books

Cook, Stephen, Ed. *ECOOP '89 Proceedings.* **Cambridge University Press, 1989.**
Proceedings of the third annual ECOOP (European Conference on Object-Oriented Programming).

Gjessing, Stein and Kristen Nygaard, Editors. *ECOOP '88 Proceedings (as Volume 322 of Lecture Notes in Computer Science).* **Springer-Verlag, 1988.**
Proceedings of the second annual ECOOP (European Conference on Object-Oriented Programming).

Krasner, Glenn, ed. *Smalltalk-80: Bits of History, Words of Advice.* **Addison-Wesley, 1983.**
For implementers and the curious.

Meyer, Bertrand. *Object-oriented Software Construction.* **Prentice Hall, 1988.**
(See notes above under Intermediate.)

Meyerowitz, Norman, ed.
OOPSLA '86 Proceedings. **ACM, 1986.**
OOPSLA '87 Proceedings. **ACM, 1987.**
OOPSLA '88 Proceedings. **ACM, 1988.**
OOPSLA '89 Proceedings. **ACM, 1989.**
ECOOP/OOPSLA '90 Proceedings. **ACM, 1990.**
Proceedings of the annual ACM OOPSLA conferences. (OOPSLA stands for Object-Oriented Programming Systems, Languages, and Applications). Also published as ACM SIGPLAN Notices issues. Recent issues also available through ACM Press - Addison-Wesley.

Paepcke, A., ed. *OOPSLA '91 Proceedings.* **ACM, 1991.**
Proceedings of the 1991 annual ACM OOPSLA conference in Phoenix in October 1991. Also published as ACM SIGPLAN Notices issues and available through ACM Press - Addison-Wesley.

Peterson, ed. *Object-Oriented Computing.*
Volume 1: Concepts;
Volume 2: Implementations.
IEEE Computer Society Press, 1988.
Another in a long series of excellent IEEE paper collections, this time on OOPS. The papers included survey the field well; included are most of the papers from the famous August 1981 *Byte*, the first public description of Smalltalk-80.

Stroustrup, Bjorn. *The* C++ *Programming Language.*
Addison-Wesley, 1986, and a second edition in 1990.
The C++ reference book. Not an introduction to C++ or OOPS.

Books on Design and Analysis

Booch, Grady. *Object-Oriented Design, with Applications.*
Benjamin/Cummings, 1991.
How to design complex object-oriented systems. Examples in
Smalltalk, Object Pascal, C++, Common Lisp Object System, and
Ada. Contains extensive bibliography.

Coad, Peter and Edward Yourdon. *Object-Oriented Analysis.*
Yourdon Press, 1990.
Analysis of systems using OO techniques.

Mullin, Mark. *Object-oriented Program Design.* Addison-
Wesley, 1989.
Good introduction to object-oriented program design, with
examples in C++.

Rumbaugh, James, Mechael Blaha, William Premerlani,
Frederick Eddy, and William Lorensen. *Object-Oriented
Modeling and Design.* Prentice Hall, 1991.
A notation and system for high level design of object-oriented
systems.

Wirfs-Brock, Rebecca, Brian Wilkerson, Lauren Wiener.
Designing Object-Oriented Software. Prentice Hall, 1990.
A language independent OOP design methodology with several
example designs.

Periodicals

C++ *Report.*
Published 10 times a year. C++ Report, c/o SIGS Publications,
Inc., 310 Madison Avenue, NY, NY 10017.

Hotline on Object-oriented Programming (HOOT).
Published biweekly. Expensive; get your company library to
subscribe. HOOT, c/o SIGS Publications, Inc., 310 Madison
Avenue, NY, NY 10017.

Journal of Object-Oriented Programming.
Published bimonthly. Known as JOOP. Contains articles and
papers about OOP, and lots of product advertising along with
columns on most languages. Tends to be more formal than *Object*.

Journal of Object-Oriented Programming, c/o SIGS Publications, Inc., 310 Madison Avenue, NY, NY 10017.

Object.

Contains articles about OOP, and lots of product advertising along with columns on most languages. Less formal than *JOOP*. *Object*, c/o SIGS Publications, Inc., 310 Madison Avenue, NY, NY 10017.

OOPS Messenger.

Published by the ACM Special Interest Group on Programming Languages (SIGPlan). Available to ACM and SIGPlan members through normal subscription methods; nonmembers write: Association for Computing Machinery, 11 West 42nd Street, New York, NY 10036 or call (212) 869-7440.

B

Procedural Programming

Procedural programming is the term used to describe programming done in conventional programming languages such as C, Pascal., FORTRAN, or COBOL. Specialized languages such as LISP, Prolog, and Snobol may have procedural components but are based on yet other metaphors.

Procedural programs have four characteristics of interest:

* Code and data are separate concepts;
* Data types are built into the language;
* Programs are designed around code structure; and
* Related function is distributed through many modules.

Code and Data Are Separate

Code and data are defined separately. The names of procedures and global data must be unique, and must not conflict with each other.

Procedures operate on data and are designed and coded separately from the definitions of the data on which they operate.

Example

There must be only one procedure named **stateTax** or **sort**, and only one set of data named **stateTaxTable**.

The procedure **stateTax** operates on **stateTaxTable** but the two are defined separately, and **stateTaxTable** could be known to other procedures.

Problem

Data cannot be tied to code that operates on it. Code thus can be called, passing the wrong data. Worse, data can be accessed from other code; changes to data become uncontrolled in large, older systems, where no one knows where a particular data item is being changed, nor why.

Since data cannot be protected from change by other procedures, authors of those other procedures will take advantage of the ability to access, especially in situations of rushed schedules or critical bug fixes. Taking a quick look into a table or control block from code that was not supposed to access that data is easy, and at the time seems all too reasonable.

Data Types Built into Languages

Data must be one of a few predefined types, or arrays or structures of these types. Most languages implement integers and floating point numbers. Most do not implement complex numbers, vectors, calculations with physical units (meters, grams, etc.), zip codes, latitudes or longitudes, phone numbers, and so on.

The data types are known to the language and further must be specified by the programmer for each procedure and variable.

Examples

A sort routine is known to take a specific type for its inputs and to produce a specific data type as a result.

A search routine must know details of the table (or other structure) it is to search.

Problem

There are at once too many data types and yet not enough. Too many because one has to specify parameters and arrays as being of a specific type; the ability to write general library routines is thus compromised. Too few because only those the language designer liked are present; if a needed type, such as complex, or a needed collection, such as a set, are missing then they cannot be added.

Typing of parameters to and results from library routines results in either a proliferation of library routines (return sorted array of integers, return sorted array of floats, return sorted array of pointers to array of strings, etc.), or the lack of needed library routines.

Worse, predefined types act as blinders. For example, since languages typically provide arrays as the only method of holding a group of like data, users rarely think of solving problems with other kinds of groupings such as:

sets
   non-indexed, only one of each thing; useful, for example, when accumulating names or part numbers for a complete list; or

queues
   ordered collections with front and/or back, and push and pop operations; useful in any application where the size of data can grow, elements can be added or removed, or stack or queue properties are needed; or

dictionaries
   keyed collections; useful when a key (name or part number) is associated with data about it (address or part information).

If these are needed, they must typically be built from arrays and specific to the situation at hand, because of the impossibility of building general purpose library routines.

In addition, any real world data item has to be represented as one of the predefined data types or a combination. For example, a zip code (postal code) in the USA is often represented as an integer, a decimal number, or a string of 5 digits. These are all forced fits since zip codes are not really numbers. Adding or subtracting from a zip code is meaningless but is an available operation.

Designed around Code Structure

Whether or not top-down design is used, the structure of procedural programs is code-based, not data-based, since one writes code, not data.

The structure of the program depends on the use envisioned when it was first written. Conventional design finds the "top" of the program, and then codes by successive refinement. The choice of "top" will greatly affect the final program structure.[28]

Example

A program designed for an interactive teletype environment (as in traditional timesharing) is structured with a command read loop at the top which reads the user's commands and then executes them. Each command may require further input data which it requests from the user as it needs it, or sometimes all at once as it starts up.

Each command may have subroutines which require data differently from each other. Again, these request data as they are run.

More modern interactive systems, such as OS/2 Presentation Manager or the Macintosh, separate the interactions which provide input data from those that perform calculations. Control is event driven, which means that it depends on what the user does with the keyboard and mouse. The user can select a particular set of calculations to perform (corresponding roughly to a "command") and is then shown by which inputs and options are needed by which fields and controls remain active or become active.

Unlike with timesharing, the interface is most often always active, with the currently active controls being easily recognized and with results of calculations, or indication of progress, being highly visible.

The underlying structure of the two programs is very different.

Problem

The structure of code reflects a solution to a problem. Traditional approaches to determining the structure involve finding the "top" and then evolving the program by some process such as step-wise refinement.

The top in interactive, text-based systems is the command read loop. Thus the basic structure of the solution is based on a particular operating system approach to serving users, not to the problem itself.

Bottom-up designs involve finding a set or sets of operations that are basic to the program and then writing routines to implement them. Some top-down approach is then used to connect the routines.

In either of these approaches the emphasis is on the way that the code is structured, not on the data the program operates on. This impacts reusability directly, since code that relates to the data and how it is used is much more apt to be able to be used again.

Distributed Functionality

Routines know too much about other routines. Changes to one routine force changes in other routines.

Example

A zip code defined as 5 decimal digits cannot simply be changed to 9 digits to reflect the newer extended zip code length. The original 5-digit portion is unchanged; the additional 4 digits really make a zip code be a structure of two fields. Making that change requires changing every line of code that refers to the 5-digit value.

Example

The routine below (written in a pseudo-code similar to C) calculates the salary, given an employee data record. It knows about the three kinds of employees. Every time a new employee type is added, this routine and each other routine having such a case statement must be found, modified, and compiled. What should be a simple change ripples through the program causing changes (and new bugs) throughout.

```
procedure earn( structure emp e )
  switch( e->type ) {
    case REGULAR:       return e->salary;
    case EXECUTIVE:     return e->salary + e->bonus;
    case SALESPERSON:   return e->salary + e->comm;
  end switch;
end procedure
```

Problem

Information about the data type, the employee record in this case, is distributed throughout the program.

Details about the kinds of employees, the shapes of visual objects, the types of products sold, the models of a product, are all things that change and should not become hard-coded into the structure of programs.

Yet conventional programming provides no other way to handle such information except to make it explicitly visible.

Code Reuse

Very little code written in conventional languages can be reused even in similar situations.[29]

Problem

Code reuse has long been a goal but one not achieved. In conventional languages it is not possible to write a general purpose sort routine and place it into a library. Instead, one has a long list of special purpose sort routines for sorting arrays of integers, long integers, floats, etc. If the language supported other kinds of collections, like lists or queues, then each collection type would force another set of routines for sorting integer lists, etc.

Summary

We've discussed five different problems with conventional languages. Each of these is real and troublesome. Each of these has been with us so long that many of us have taken them to be part of the definition of how computing works.

We think that it is just the way things are when we have to write yet another table search or sort routine.

We accept that there is little code reuse.

We accept that people tend to code immediately instead of designing. We come up with design systems which force design first, except that the forcing is really through management edict. Programmers do it because it is "good for them" not because they necessarily believe in it.

Things don't have to be the way they are. OOP provides proof that other ways of programming can solve many of these problems. [30]

This glossary briefly defines the terms used in this book. When a definition uses a term also defined in this glossary it is shown in boldface. Terms that are class names or parts of the Smalltalk language are shown in the code typeface (`like this`.)

abstract class
abstract superclass

A parent **class** or **superclass** which is created for its **protocol** alone. It is not intended that **instances** exist. It is intended that the abstract class act as a model for a **subclass** or subclasses, defining the minimum **protocol** that they must support.

access method

A **method** that provides access to an **instance variable**. The access may return or set the value.

binary

One of the three forms of **message selector** in **Smalltalk**; see also **unary** and **keyword**. Binary messages are distinguished by a message selector formed from one or two special characters, and have one **input**.

For example:

    `2 + 3`   Binary message (+) and one input (3).

    `a < b`   Binary message (<) and one input (b)

block

A group of Smalltalk statements enclosed in square braces: `[...]`. A block is an **object**. It can be assigned or passed as an input to another block or a method. It can take zero or more inputs.

C++

A popular **OOP** language, an extension of the C language.

class

The definition of an **object**. A class contains the list of data that will be in each **instance** of the object, the **method**s that will act on that data, and methods that belong to the class itself. (See **class method**.)

class hierarchy

See **hierarchy**.

class method

A **method** that belongs to the **class** itself. These methods typically are used to allocate new instances. Class methods can (and often do) have the same names as **instance methods**. (Also see **new.**)

class variable

A variable belonging to a **class**. It can be referenced by an **instance method** or a **class method**. It is thus global to the class and its **subclass**es.

Collection

A **class** that comes with **Smalltalk**. It is an **abstract class** that defines **protocol** for a number of **subclass**es. The subclasses define a number of different ways to collect data and access the collected data.

data hiding

See **encapsulation**.

ECOOP

The European Conference on Object-Oriented Programming. An annual conference.

encapsulation

Hiding data behind a wall of code. In pure **OOP** languages no data can be accessed except by code (**methods**) defined along with that data. The data and associated methods are defined together and are called a **class**.

false

The name, in **Smalltalk**, for the not-true condition. The result of evaluating 2=3 is always **false**. (See **true**.)

hierarchy

A related set of concepts, working from the more general (higher in the hierarchy) to the more specific (lower in the hierarchy.) The more specific concepts are said to inherit from the more general. (See **inheritance**.)

In **Smalltalk**, the hierarchy is used to define **class**es, with classes higher in the hierarchy having more abstract characteristics (and sometimes being **abstract class**es) and those lower in the hierarchy being more specific. The bottom levels of the hierarchy represent executable classes.

inheritance

The process of obtaining characteristics from a parent in a **hierarchy**. Characteristics that can be inherited in **OOP** are **instance variables**, **instance methods**, **class variables**, and **class methods**.

input

A parameter to a **method**. A name in the method refers to the value of the input.

instance

The data defined by a **class** plus a reference to the class. An instance holds the data; the class holds the code; the class reference in the instance lets **message**s find the appropriate **method** when a message is sent.

Instances are also called **objects**.

instance method

A **method** in a **class** that is executed when a **message** is sent to an **instance**.

instance variable

The data in an **instance**, listed and named in the defining **class**, is a list of instance variables.

keyword

One of the three forms of **message selector** in **Smalltalk**; see also **unary** and **binary**. Keyword messages are distinguished by a message selector formed from names ended with a colon. Each keyword selector can have multiple parts, one per input.

For example:

at:	One colon; one input.
at:put:	Two colons; two inputs.
at:put:with:	Three colons; three inputs.

message

That which is sent to an **instance** (or `class`) to execute a **method**. A message has the same name as the method that is to be run. See **message selector** and **message lookup**.

message selector

> The name of a **message**. The selector can be **unary**, **binary**, or **keyword**.

message lookup

> The process whereby a **method** is found when a **message** is sent. The message lookup first tries to find a method with a matching name in the **class** of the **instance** to which the message is first sent, then in its **superclass**, etc. (But see **super** for an exception.)

message send

> The act of sending a **message**.

method

> A subroutine or procedure that belongs to a **class** and which is run by a **message send**. A method, once found, is executed just as if it were a subroutine in a conventional language. That which makes a method special is the **message lookup**.

method header

> The first line(s) of a **method** which defines the method name, form (**keyword**, **binary**, or **unary**), and **input**s.

method lookup

> See **message lookup**.

new

> The **message** sent to a **class** to get an **instance**.

object

> Another name for **instance**.

Object

> The name of the **class** in **Smalltalk** which is at the top of the class **hierarchy**. All other classes are **subclass**es. **Object** can be thought of as the highest level **abstract superclass**.

object-oriented programming

> A method of programming involving four characteristics: **encapsulation**, **hierarchy** of definitions, **polymorphism**, and a **single type**.

OOP

> Slang, or shorthand, for **object-oriented programming**.

OOPS

Slang, or shorthand, for **object-oriented programming system**.

OOPSLA

Object-Oriented Programming Systems, Languages, and Applications. An annual conference sponsored by ACM and SIGPlan.

override

Replace an inherited **method** with another method of the same name at a lower level in the **hierarchy**.

parameter

See **input**.

polymorphism

Literally, having multiple names. In **OOP** it means that **method**s in different classes can have the same name. **Inheritance** separates some identically named methods from each other. The **message lookup** process resolves which of the remaining identically named methods to run.

protocol

1) The list of **method**s supported by a **class**.

2) A coherent subset of the list of methods supported by a class. If a new class supports the same methods as does, say, class `Collection`, then it can be said to have the `Collection` protocol.

self

The name of an **object** as known by its methods. That is, within a **method** the object for which that method is running is known by the name `self`. (Also see **super**.)

single type

A variable in **OOP** can hold anything; that is, the kind of thing that a variable can hold is not specified. It is thus said that there is but one type: an **object**.

Smalltalk

An **OOP** language that has evolved and developed into one of the current set of commercial OOP languages. It is almost unique among such languages in that it is based purely on **object-oriented** concepts rather than an add-on to a more conventional language.

subclass

> A **class** based on another class in the **hierarchy**. It is said to **inherit** from its **superclass** (its parent.)

super

> Another name of an **object** as known by its methods. (See **self**.)
>
> When the object is referred to by **super**, the **method lookup** changes. Instead of looking in the **instance methods** of the **class** of the object, the first class searched is the **superclass** of the class in which the current method is contained.

superclass

> 1) A class which has a **subclass**.
>
> 2) The parent of a class.

true

> The name, in **Smalltalk**, for the not-false condition. The result of evaluating 2=2 is always **true**. See **false**.

unary

> One of the three forms of **message selector** in **Smalltalk**; see also **binary** and **keyword**. Unary messages are distinguished by a message selector formed from words. It has no **input**s, and thus no colons in the name.
>
> For example:
>
> | | |
> |------------|----------------------------|
> | angle sin | Send the **sin** message. |
> | x sqrt | Send the **sqrt** message. |

variable

> In **Smalltalk** there are four kinds of variables:
>
> 1) **instance variable**s which hold the data in **object**s;
>
> 2) **class variable**s which are global to a **class** and its **subclasses**;
>
> 3) **input** variables (or parameters) to **method**s and **block**s; and
>
> 4) temporary variables which exist for the execution of a single method.

Notes

1   Stroustrup, B. (1986). *The C++ Programming Language.* New York, Addison-Wesley.

2   Cox, B. (1986). Object-Oriented Programming - An Evolutionary Approach. New York, Addison-Wesley.

3   Goldberg and Robson. (1983). *Smalltalk-80: The Language and Its Implementation.* New York, Addison-Wesley.

4   Kirkerud, B. (1989). *Object-Oriented Programming with Simula.* Wokingham, England, Addison-Wesley.

5   Krasner. (1983). *Smalltalk-80: Bits of History, Words of Advice.* New York, Addison-Wesley.

6   Deutsch, L. P. (1989). "The Past, Present, and Future of Smalltalk." ECOOP '89. : 73-87.

7   Digitalk. (1987, 1989). *Smalltalk/V.* Los Angeles, Digitalk.
Digitalk. (1988). *Smalltalk/V-286.* Los Angeles, Digitalk.
Digitalk. (1989). *Smalltalk/V-PM.* Los Angeles, Digitalk.

8   Hewett. (1977). "Viewing Control Structures as Patterns of Passing Messages." (June, 1977): 323-364.

9   Goldberg and Robson. (1983). *Smalltalk-80: The Language and Its Implementation.* New York, Addison-Wesley.

10   Goldberg and Robson. (1989). *Smalltalk-80: The Language.* New York, Addison-Wesley.

11   Actually, some systems implement only some of the base characteristics and there can be argument about whether the resulting system is object-oriented or not.

12   The last characteristic, single type, is controversial. Some prefer to stress the concept of dynamic binding.

I consider that the concept of a single type encompasses the concept of dynamic binding, since the language implementation cannot tell what is in a variable until a message is sent to it.

Others prefer to think of variables in Smalltalk as having no type, but instead think of the data as having type. This is a fun distinction to make, and have arguments about, but the effect is the same.

Some languages that are called Object Oriented require that variables be typed, or partly typed, or declared as holding an object of unknown type. Some think of these languages as only partly Object Oriented and some as fully Object Oriented. The conclusion one draws often depends on ones favorite language.

13   Some people prefer to think of variables as having no type and the data as having type instead. The result is the same, though, however one prefers to think of it.

In some OOP languages variables are typed and as a result some people don't think these languages are fully object oriented. Often there is a way to specify that a given variable can hold any object though.

14   In many languages a variable can have an associated type. One might define a new type for color and then specify that the variable color has that type. The association of a type with the name would seemingly make the variable name have meaning; however one could still call a variable with the color type by any name, even **weight** or **price**.

15   From surveys made by the organizers of OOPSLA conferences.

16   See Appendix A for information on these vendors.

17   In Smalltalk, as in many other OOP languages, arithmetic and relational operators such as + or > are also implemented as messages to objects. Thus **2+3** sends the **+** message to the **2** passing the **3** as an input. We'll get back to this a bit later when we need to write such methods.

18   More formally, a period is a statement separator in Smalltalk, not a statement terminator. Unlike Pascal, however, it is quite obvious where periods need to go.

19   More generally, upper-case variables really are global and others are local to some scope such as an instance or a method execution. Most global variables are simply class definitions; global variables are good for little else (and are bad practice for most other things).

20   The order of evaluation of expressions in Smalltalk is:

(1)   Unary messages are first.

(2)   Operators (binary messages) are evaluated next, left to right. Thus **2 + 3 + 4** is equivalent to **(2 + 3) + 4**.

(3)   Keyword messages are evaluated last.

Thus this expression:

    emp salary: emp salary + raise

is evaluated as if it had been written:

    emp salary: ((emp salary) + raise)

The **salary** message is sent to **emp**, the **+** message is sent to the returned value passing **raise**, and then the **salary:** message is sent to **emp** passing the result returned by the **+** message.

21   In Smalltalk-80 an up arrow is used:

```
currentLoad
    ↑ curLoad
```

22   This is not true in most other OOP systems, which treat classes as special things; however, most have some way for user code to control allocation of new objects.

23   The last four lines in the definition can be written as one using a Smalltalk feature called cascading:

```
Class Methods:
mass: z
    (z <= 0)  ifTrue: [ (error message) ].
    ^(Ball new) mass: z; velocity: 0
```

In the last line, a new instance of **Ball** is obtained; then the mass is set by sending the **mass:** message to the new instance. The semicolon after **mass:** causes the following message, **velocity:**, to be sent to the same object as the prior message (i.e., the new instance of **Ball**). Thus the sequence of events is: get a new ball, send **mass:** to the new ball, send **velocity:** to the new ball, and then return the new ball.

24   Typographical conventions are: class names in bold are ones written in this book and others come with Smalltalk; class names in italics are abstract superclasses. Thus *Object* is an abstract superclass that comes with Smalltalk and **Ball** can have instances and is defined in this book.

25   Ashe, J. (1986). Personal communication.

26   Coad, P. and E. Yourdon. (1990). *Object-Oriented Analysis.* Englewood Cliffs, NJ, Yourdon Press, Prentice-Hall.

Rumbaug, J., M. Blaha, W. Premerlani, F. Eddy and W. Lorensen. (1991). *Object-Oriented Modelling and Design.* Englewood Cliffs, Prentice Hall.

Booch, G. (1991). *Object-Oriented Design.* Redwood City, California, Benjamin/Cummings.

27   Brooks, Fred. No Silver Bullet. *IEEE Computer* , April 1987.

28   See the following book for a long discussion of this topic:

Meyer. (1988). *Object-oriented Software Construction.* Englewood Cliffs, Prentice Hall.

29   On occasion, it is possible to take an existing body of code and use it as the basis for another, similar, program. However, extensive modifications are always needed and the savings is often

little. The real cost in a system are in debugging and maintaining. Real reuse occurs when existing code can be used without modification.

30   For a longer discussion of problems in conventional languages see:

Meyer. (1988). *Object-oriented Software Construction*. Englewood Cliffs, Prentice Hall.

Index

About the Author

David N. Smith is a Senior Programmer and researcher at IBM's Thomas J Watson Research Center. He has twenty-five years of experience in the computing field as a researcher, systems programmer, and project manager. He has been involved with object-oriented programming since 1983, and has presented tutorials introducing the subject at several major ACM conferences. He is a founder and member of the executive committee of the ACM Object-Oriented Programming, Systems, Languages and Applications conference (OOPSLA.)